BASIC
PRINCIPLES
OF
CURRICULUM
AND
INSTRUCTION

BASIC
PRINCIPLES
OF
CURRICULUM
AND
INSTRUCTION

Ralph W. Tyler

THE UNIVERSITY OF CHICAGO PRESS

Chicago and London

Originally Published as Syllabus for Education 360

International Standard Book Number: 0-226-82031-9

Library of Congress Catalog Card Number: A51-3967

The University of Chicago Press, Chicago 60637
The University of Chicago Press, Ltd., London

CONTENTS

INTRODUCTION

This small book attempts to explain a rationale for viewing, analyzing and interpreting the curriculum and instructional program of an educational institution. It is not a textbook, for it does not provide comprehensive guidance and readings for a course. It is not a manual for curriculum construction since it does not describe and outline in detail the steps to be taken by a given school or college that seeks to build a curriculum. This book outlines one way of viewing an instructional program as a functioning instrument of education. The student is encouraged to examine other rationales and to develop his own conception of the elements and relationships involved in an effective curriculum.

The rationale developed here begins with identifying four fundamental questions which must be answered in developing any curriculum and plan of instruction. These are:

B.O. 1. What educational purposes should the school seek to attain?

L.E. 2. What educational experiences can be provided that are likely to attain these purposes?

Organize 3. How can these educational experiences be effectively organized?

Evaluate 4. How can we determine whether these purposes are being attained?

Ques. book is involved with

This book suggests methods for studying these questions. No attempt is made to answer these questions since the answers will vary to some extent from one level of educa-

1

tion to another and from one school to another. Instead of answering the questions, an explanation is given of procedures by which these questions can be answered. This constitutes a rationale by which to examine problems of curriculum and instruction.

1 WHAT EDUCATIONAL PURPOSES SHOULD THE SCHOOL SEEK TO ATTAIN?

Ques. #1

Many educational programs do not have clearly defined purposes. In some cases one may ask a teacher of science, of English, of social studies, or of some other subject what objectives are being aimed at and get no satisfactory reply. The teacher may say in effect that he aims to develop a well-educated person and that he is teaching English or social studies or some other subject because it is essential to a well-rounded education. No doubt some excellent educational work is being done by artistic teachers who do not have a clear conception of goals but do have an intuitive sense of what is good teaching, what materials are significant, what topics are worth dealing with and how to present material and develop topics effectively with students. Nevertheless, if an educational program is to be planned and if efforts for continued improvement are to be made, it is very necessary to have some conception of the goals that are being aimed at. These educational objectives become the criteria by which materials are selected, content is outlined, instructional procedures are developed and tests and examinations are prepared. All aspects of the educational program are really means to accomplish basic educational purposes. Hence, if we are to study an educational program systematically and intelligently we must first be sure as to the educational objectives aimed at.

But how are objectives obtained? Since they are consciously willed goals, that is, ends that are desired by the school staff, are they not simply matters of personal preference of individuals or groups? Is there any place for a

3

systematic attack upon the problem of what objectives to seek?

It is certainly true that in the final analysis objectives are matters of choice, and they must therefore be the considered value judgments of those responsible for the school. A comprehensive philosophy of education is necessary to guide in making these judgments. And, in addition, certain kinds of information and knowledge provide a more intelligent basis for applying the philosophy in making decisions about objectives. If these facts are available to those making decisions, the probability is increased that judgments about objectives will be wise and that the school goals will have greater significance and greater validity. For this reason, a large part of the so-called scientific study of the curriculum during the past thirty years has concerned itself with investigations that might provide a more adequate basis for selecting objectives wisely. The technical literature of the curriculum field includes hundreds of studies that collected information useful to curriculum groups in selecting objectives.

Accepting the principle that investigations can be made which will provide information and knowledge useful in deciding about objectives, the question is then raised what sources can be used for getting information that will be helpful in this way. A good deal of controversy goes on between essentialists and progressives, between subject specialists and child psychologists, between this group and that school group over the question of the basic source from which objectives can be derived. The progressive emphasizes the importance of studying the child to find out what kinds of interests he has, what problems he encounters, what purposes he has in mind. The progressive sees this information as providing the basic source for selecting objectives. The essentialist, on the other hand, is impressed by the large body of knowledge collected over many thousands of years, the so-called cultural heritage, and emphasizes this as the primary source for deriving objectives. The essentialist views objectives as essentially the basic learnings selected from the vast cultural heritage of the past.

Many sociologists and others concerned with the pressing problems of contemporary society see in an analysis of contemporary society the basic information from which objectives can be derived. They view the school as the agency for helping young people to deal effectively with the critical problems of contemporary life. If they can determine what these contemporary problems are then the objectives of the school are to provide those knowledges, skills, attitudes, and the like that will help people to deal intelligently with these contemporary problems. On the other hand, the educational philosophers recognize that there are basic values in life, largely transmitted from one generation to another by means of education. They see the school as aiming essentially at the transmission of the basic values derived by comprehensive philosophic study and hence see in educational philosophy the basic source from which objectives can be derived.

The point of view taken in this course is that no single source of information is adequate to provide a basis for wise and comprehensive decisions about the objectives of the school. Each of these sources has certain values to commend it. Each source should be given some consideration in planning any comprehensive curriculum program. Hence, we shall turn to each of the sources in turn to consider briefly what kinds of information can be obtained from the source and how this information may suggest significant educational objectives.

Studies of the Learners Themselves as a Source of Educational Objectives

Education is a process of changing the behavior patterns

of people. This is using behavior in the broad sense to include thinking and feeling as well as overt action. When education is viewed in this way, it is clear that educational objectives, then, represent the kinds of changes in behavior that an educational institution seeks to bring about in its students. A study of the learners themselves would seek to identify needed changes in behavior patterns of the students which the educational institution should seek to produce.

An investigation of children in the elementary school in a certain community may reveal dietary deficiency and inadequate physical condition. These facts may suggest objectives in health education and in social studies but they suggest objectives only when viewed in terms of some conception of normal or desirable physical condition. In a society which takes dietary deficiencies for granted, there would be little likelihood of inferring any educational objectives from such data. Correspondingly, studies of adolescence during the depression indicated that a considerable number were greatly pertrubed over the possibility that they would be unable to find work upon graduation. This does not automatically suggest the need for vocational guidance or occupational preparation. Studies of the learner suggest educational objectives only when the information about the learner is compared with some desirable standards, some conception of acceptable norms, so that the difference between the present condition of the learner and the acceptable norm can be identified. This difference or gap is what is generally referred to as a need.

There is another sense in which the term "need" is used in the psychological writings of Prescott, Murray, and others. They view a human being as a dynamic organism, an energy system normally in equilibrium between internal forces produced by the energy of the oxidation of food and external conditions. To keep the system in equilibrium it is necessary that certain "needs" be met. That is, certain tensions are produced which result in disequilibrium un-less these tensions are relieved. In this sense every organism is continually meeting its needs, that is, reacting in such a way as to relieve these forces that bring about imbalance. In these terms one of the problems of education is to chan-nel the means by which these needs are met so that the re-sulting behavior is socially acceptable, yet at the same time the needs are met and the organism is not under continu-ous, unrelieved tensions. Prescott classifies these needs into three types: physical needs such as the need for food, for water, for activity, for sex and the like; social needs such as the need for affection, for belonging, for status or respect from this social group; and integrative needs, the need to relate one's self to something larger and beyond one's self, that is, the need for a philosophy of life. In this sense all children have the same needs and it is the responsibility of the school as with every other social institution to help children to get these needs met in a way which is not only satisfying but provides the kind of behavior patterns that are personally and socially significant. A study of such needs in a given group of children would involve identifying those needs that are not being properly satisfied and an investigation of the role the school can play in helping children to meet these needs. This may often suggest educa-tional objectives in the sense of indicating certain knowl-edge, attitudes, skills, and the like, the development of which would help children to meet these needs more effectively. These studies may also suggest ways in which the school can help to give motivation and meaning to its activities by providing means for children to meet psycho-logical needs that are not well satisfied outside the school.

It is well to keep these two meanings of the term "needs" distinct so that they will not be confused in our discussion. The first use of the term represents a gap between some conception of a desirable norm, that is, some standard of

② Need - tensions that must be brought into equilibrium

philosophic value and the actual status. Need in this sense 'is the gap between what is and what should be. The other use of the term by some psychologists represents tensions in the organism which must be brought into equilibrium for a normal healthy condition of the organism to be maintained.

A large number of investigations has been carried on during the last ten or fifteen years to identify needs of students. Many of them use the term "need" in the first sense and have consisted essentially of studies aimed to find out the present status of students in terms of factors that are accepted as desirable norms. This information about the student is then compared with these norms and gaps identified in this way. Studies of needs in the psychological sense have also been conducted particularly by students of so-called "dynamic" psychology.

The argument for considering the needs of students as an important source for educational objectives runs somewhat as follows: The day-by-day environment of young people in the home and in the community generally provides a considerable part of the educational development of the student. It is unnecessary for the school to duplicate educational experiences already adequately provided outside the school. The school's efforts should be focused particularly upon serious gaps in the present development of students. Hence, studies that identify these gaps, these educational needs, are necessary studies to provide a basis for the selection of objectives which should be given primary emphasis in the school's program. Most of these studies will have two parts, first, finding the present status of the students, and second, comparing this status to acceptable norms in order to identfy the gaps or needs.

If a school is to make a comprehensive investigation of the needs of its students, several difficulties are encountered. In the first place, the needs of students may fall in any aspect of life. It is difficult to study all aspects of life simultaneously or in a single investigation. Hence, it is generally desirable to analyze life into some major aspects and investigate each of these major aspects in turn. For example, in studying the needs of children in a junior high school in Smithville the staff might profitably break down the investigation into the following phases: (1) health, (2) immediate social relationships, including life in the family and with friends and acquaintances, (3) socio-civic relationships, including the civic life of the school and the community, (4) the consumer aspects of life, (5) occupational life, and (6) recreational. These are not the only categories which might be used or are the necessarily the best, but they illustrate the division of all of the younster's life into aspects each of which can be investigated more conveniently. For each of these aspects of life, the investigation might properly include studies of the child's practices, knowledge and ideas, attitudes, interests, and the like. For example, in the case of health study, the investigation might go into such health practices as food habits, habits relating to rest and relaxation, habits of cleanliness, practices relating to safety and protection of the health of others, present health knowledge, and misconceptions students have about facts of health and hygiene, attitudes toward the importance of personal health and their responsibility for the protection of health of others, interests in learning more about the field of health. Investigations of this sort can give a great deal of information about the present status of children in the school so far as health is concerned. This information would then need to be compared with some set of desirable norms in order to identify serious gaps which in turn would suggest educational objectives.

In studying the needs of the learners, certain data will be found to be common to most children of that age level whether they live in one part of the country or another, whether they are rural or city children, whether they are of one social class or another. On the other hand, there are other facts which would vary quite markedly from one school to another and from one group in the school to another group. For example, the health habits and knowledge, the skills in reading, writing and mathematics, the knowledge of socio-civic affairs, and attitudes toward social institutions will vary markedly among schools. Hence, a school that is making an investigation will find it possible to draw upon general scientific studies for certain information about children of the age level concerned, but it will be necessary to supplement this general information by studies of the particular students within the particular school concerned, and in making these investigations it will often be necessary to recognize the varied composition in the student body representing the typical school. It is possible then to identify some needs that are common to most American children, other needs that are common to almost all of the children in the given school, and still other needs that are common to certain groups within the school but not common to a majority of the children in the school.

To get a clear picture of the needs of learners, I would suggest that you consider the school with which you are most familiar and that you outline particular investigations that could be carried on in that school to give you the kind of information about the needs of students which would throw some light on objectives for that school.

Another type of study of the learner, which demands particular consideration, is the investigation of students interests. A good deal of publicity has been given to the purported theory of progressive education that the primary basis for educational objectives is the interests of the learners themselves. According to this idea, children's interests must be identified so that they can serve as the focus of educational attention.

Probably no thoughtful proponent of progressive education ever advocated teaching students only the things in which they were at that moment interested, but the argument for using studies of student interests as a basis for objectives runs somewhat as follows: Education is an active process. It involves the active efforts of the learner himself. In general, the learner learns only those things which he does. If the school situations deal with matters of interest to the learner he will actively participate in them and thus learn to deal effectively with these situations. Furthermore, it is argued that the increasing effectiveness with which he handles present situations guarantees his ability to meet new situations as they arise. Hence, it is essential to see that education provides opportunities for the student to enter actively into, and to deal wholeheartedly with, the things which interest him, and in which he is deeply involved, and to learn particularly how to carry on such activities effectively.

There are many educators who do not consider attention to the present interest of students as an adequate educational program because one of the functions of education is to broaden and deepen the student's interest so that he will continue his education long after he has ended his formal school training. But even these educators recognize the value of beginning with present student interests as a point of departure. Hence, various groups conduct investigations of student interests to throw light upon the possible educational objectives of the school. Where these interests are desirable ones they provide the starting point for effective instruction. Where the interests are undesirable, narrow, limited or inadequate, they indicate gaps which need to be overcome if the student is to receive an effective education.

A great many studies have been made of children's interests in various fields. Craig, for example, made a study of the questions children asked about science and developed a curriculum in elementary school science, aimed primarily at providing the basis upon which children could answer questions in which they were interested. Studies have been made of children's interests in reading, and the curriculum in literature has sometimes been developed in terms of children's reading interests. Interests in games and sports have been used as a basis for setting up objectives in the physical education fields. In studying interests as well as in studying needs, the possible interests are so varied that it usually is necessary to plan a series of investigations into the various phases of student interests rather than to make a single study which attempts to cover all the aspects of life in which students may have interests of one sort or another. For example, an investigation may be made of children's interests in health, another of interests in family activities, and so on.

To get a clearer idea of the possible value to be obtained from studies of student interests, I would suggest that you outline a plan for the study of student interests that could be made in the school with which you are most familiar. This might indicate to what degree you could draw upon previous studies of children's interests where interests were likely to be very universal and what other areas of interests you would need to study locally, in your own community or in your own school, because the variations from one group of children to another in these areas would be great enough so that the results of other investigations would not be a dependable indication of the interests that exist in your school.

What methods can be used in studying the learner? Almost all of the methods of social investigation can be employed in studying the learner's needs and interests. In some cases observations by the teacher will establish a good many facts about students, particularly about their school activities, their social relations, their school habits and the like. A second source is the student interview which because it is time-consuming can be used generally on only a sample of students. The interview, however, develops an opportunity to get more informal data about how students feel about things, their attitudes, their interests, their philosophy of life and the like. Parent interviews are helpful in throwing further light upon certain health practices and social relations of students. The questionnaire is a useful device for getting information which the student has no hesitation in providing. Interest questionnaires have been very widely used as well as questionnaires about recreational activities, about problems of a personal and social sort, about reading habits, health habits, work experience and the like. In a great many cases, tests have been used, particularly tests of present status in skills, like reading, writing, mathematics, in knowledge, in attitudes, and in problem-solving abilities. Furthermore, in most communities there are records which help to throw further light upon some types of student needs and interests. These include such things as records of juvenile delinquency, mortality and morbidity records with reference to health conditions, various types of social data by community, or area, within the city and the like. Of course, the initial study should be an examination of the school records, especially if the school maintains cumulative records of the students.

The repertoire of study techniques is broad enough to provide opportunity for all teachers and staff members to participate at some point in a study of student needs and interests. Furthermore, in many cases, students themselves will be interested in participating in the investigation, making a house-to-house canvass, where needed, or collecting data of other sorts in connection with a comprehensive investigation.

Some schools, who have given lip service to the use of studies of the learner, have not been able to derive educational objectives from these investigations. There is no single formula for inferring educational objectives from data about students. In general, the procedure involves studying the data to see implications, comparing the data with norms or standards in the field and from that, obtaining suggestions about possible needs that a school program could meet. The importance of sensing the implications of the data in the light of acceptable norms cannot be overemphasized because the same items of data permit several possible interpretations. For example, the discovery that 60 percent of the boys in the ninth grade of a certain high school read nothing outside of school other than the comic strips might suggest to some unimaginative teacher that the school needs to teach these boys how to read comic strips more rapidly or with greater satisfaction. On the other hand, to another teacher this would suggest the limitations of the reading interests of these boys and the need for setting up objectives gradually to broaden and deepen these reading interests. Correspondingly, the discovery that in a particular high school 90 percent of the graduates went to work immediately after graduation and did not go to college might suggest to some school that the primary objectives of this school should be to develop occupational skills so that these boys and girls could be immediately employable. On the other hand, to other teachers it would suggest the importance of doing everything possible to develop interests in social and civic matters and to get in a large segment of general education, because these young people would have so little opportunity for further formal education. You can see how the norms, that is, the philosophy of life and of education which guides the teacher, enter into the interpretation of data of this sort. Although the data have usefulness in indicating gaps and opportunities which can be given particular attention in setting up educational objectives, it is clear that the objectives are not automatically identified by collecting information about the students.

Another point of confusion in interpreting data about the learner is the failure to distinguish between the needs that are appropriately met by education and needs that are properly met through other social agencies. For example, the discovery that a considerable fraction of the student body suffers from malnutrition has both educational and noneducational implications. Insofar as the malnutrition is due to lack of knowledge of desirable diets, or lack of adequate health habits, or lack of desirable attitudes toward the importance of health the need is an educational one that can be met by developing an educational program which will bring about the necessary knowledge, habits, attitudes, and the like. On the other hand, malnutrition is often due to lack of adequate income for certain parts of the population and/or the unavailability of the food required for an effective diet. These latter cases are illustrations of social needs which cannot be met simply by educational objectives achieved in the school but require other forms of social action. In deriving objectives from studies of student needs the teacher must identify implications relevant to educational objectives and not confuse them with implications that do not relate to education, that is, he should identify desirable changes in the behavior patterns of students which would help to meet the needs indicated by the data.

To provide a thorough understanding of the possibilities of, and the difficulties involved in, drawing interpretations about educational objectives from data about student needs and interests, I would suggest that you jot down data about groups of students with whom you are familiar, formulating as comprehensive a set of data about their needs and interests as you can. Then attempt to write down the educational objectives which these data imply. Set down every suggested educational objective that comes to your mind and then see how you arrived at this objective, what other factors you took into account, how you were able to infer from these data the particular educational objectives that you did. This exercise should, I think, indicate to you both the values of concrete data about students as a basis for suggesting objectives and also the difficulties involved in interpreting such data.

Studies of Contemporary Life Outside the School

The effort to derive objectives from studies of contemporary life largely grew out of the difficulty of accomplishing all that was laid upon the schools with the greatly increased body of knowledge which developed after the advent of science and the Industrial Revolution. Prior to this time the body of material that was considered academically respectable was sufficiently small so that there was little problem in selecting the elements of most importance from the cultural heritage. With the tremendous increase in knowledge accelerating with each generation after the advent of science, the schools found it no longer possible to include in their program all that was accepted by scholars. Increasingly the question was raised as to the contemporary significance of particular items of knowledge or particular skills and abilities. Herbert Spencer in his essay on *What Knowledge is of Most Worth* attempted to deal with this problem in a way that has characterized many of the efforts over the past century. Although this represented the interpretation of informal observations rather than systematic studies, the technique used by Spencer in some respects is very similar to techniques used by investigators today.

When the first World War required the training of a large number of people in the skilled trades, training that must take place in a relatively short period of time, the older and slower apprentice systems were no longer adequate. The idea of job analysis developed and was widely used to work out training programs in World War I which would speed up the training of people for the skilled trades and various types of technology. In essence, job analysis is simply a method of analyzing the activities carried on by a worker in a particular field in order that a training program can be focused upon those critical activities performed by this worker. In essence, most studies of contemporary life have a somewhat similar "logic."

Today there are two commonly used arguments for analyzing contemporary life in order to get suggestions for educational objectives. The first of these arguments is that because contemporary life is so complex and because life is continually changing, it is very necessary to focus educational efforts upon the critical aspects of this complex life and upon those aspects that are of importance today so that we do not waste the time of students in learning things that were important fifty years ago but no longer have significance at the same time that we are neglecting areas of life that are now important and for which the schools provide no preparation.

A second argument for the study of contemporary life grows out of the findings relating to transfer of training. As long as educators believed that it was possible for a student to train his mind and the various faculties of the mind in general and that he could use these faculties under whatever conditions might be appropriate, there was less need for analyzing contemporary life to suggest objectives. According to this view the important objectives were to develop the several faculties of the mind and as life developed the student would be able to use this trained mind to meet the conditions that he encountered. Studies of transfer of training, however, indicated that the student was much more likely to apply his learning when he recognized the similarity between the situations encountered in life and the situations in which the learning took place. Furthermore, the student was more likely to perceive the similarity between the life situations and the learning situations when two conditions were met: (1) the life situations and the learning situations were obviously alike in many respects, and (2) the student was given practice in seeking illustrations in his life outside of school for the application of things learned in school. These findings are used to support the value of analyzing contemporary life to identify learning objectives for the school that can easily be related to the conditions and opportunities of contemporary life for use of these kinds of learning.

Using studies of contemporary life as a basis for deriving objectives has sometimes been criticized particularly when it is the sole basis for deriving objectives. One of the most frequent criticisms has been that the identification of contemporary activities does not in itself indicate their desirability. The finding, for example, that large numbers of people are engaged in certain activities does not per se indicate that these activities should be taught to students in the school. Some of these activities may be harmful and in place of being taught in the school some attention might need to be given to their elimination. The second type of criticism is the type made by essentialists who refer to studies of contemporary life as the cult of "presentism." These critics point out that because life is continually changing, preparing students to solve the problems of today will make them unable to deal with the problems they will encounter as adults because the problems will have changed. A third kind of criticism is that made by some progressives who point out that some of the critical problems of contemporary life and some of the common activities engaged in by adults are not in themselves interesting to children nor of concern to children, and to assume that they should become educational objectives for children of a given age neglects the importance of considering the children's interests and children's needs as a basis for deriving objectives.

These criticisms in the main apply to the derivation of objectives solely from studies of contemporary life. When objectives derived from studies of contemporary life are checked against other sources and in terms of an acceptable educational philosophy, the first criticism is removed. When studies of contemporary life are used as a basis for indicating important areas that appear to have continuing importance, and when the studies of contemporary life suggest areas in which students can have opportunity to practice what they learn in school, and also when an effort is made to develop in students an intelligent understanding of the basic principles involved in these matters, the claim that such a procedure involves a worship of "presentism" is largely eliminated. Finally, if studies of contemporary life are used to indicate directions in which educational objectives may aim, while the choice of particular objectives for given children takes into account student interests and needs, these studies of contemporary life can be useful without violating relevant criteria of appropriateness for students of particular age levels. Hence, it is worthwhile to utilize data obtained from studies of contemporary life as one source for suggesting possible educational objectives.

In making studies of life outside the school as in studying the learner, it is necessary to divide life into various phases in order to have manageable areas for investigation. Unless life is analyzed into functional and significant phases it is too big to be attacked and any effort in study will result in many gaps. There are various ways in which contemporary life may be analyzed in order to obtain manageable categories for study. As with the investigation of the learner

How contemporary life may be analyzed

One classification possible is (a) health, (b) family, (c) recreation, (d) vocation, (e) religion, (f) consumption, and (g) civic. A more detailed classification was used in the Virginia State Curriculum Study as indicated by the following headings:

(a) Protection and Conservation of Life.
(b) Natural Resources.
(c) Production of Goods and Services and Distribution of the Returns of Production.
(d) Consumption of Goods and Services.
(e) Communication and Transportation of Goods and People.
(f) Recreation.
(g) Expression of Esthetic Impulses.
(h) Expression of Religious Impulses.
(i) Education.
(j) Extension of Freedom.
(k) Integration of the Individual.
(l) Exploration.

No single classification of aspects of life is wholly satisfactory, but since the purpose is to break down a total concept of life into manageable aspects and to see that no important phrase is omitted, it is possible to use any one of a number of classifications and accomplish this end. In each phrase of life the purpose is to get information about that aspect of contemporary life which is likely to have implication for educational objectives. A good many types of information have been obtained for this purpose, for example, some studies have been made of the activities engaged in by people in this aspect of life on the general assumption that objectives of education can be inferred from activities because education should help people to carry on their activities more effectively. In other cases, investigations have been made of the critical problems in a given area, in others, studies have been made of the defects of life in particular areas including the difficulties and serious maladjustments. Some studies have made investigation of the interests, hopes, and aspirations of people in particular phases of their lives on the ground that education should help people more adequately to satisfy their interests and to achieve their hopes and aspirations. Some investigations have abtained data about the information, concepts, misconceptions, superstitions, and ideas people have on the ground that education should help people to have relevant and accurate information in a given field. Others have obtained data about the habits and skills of people in particular areas, studying the habits to see what changes in them are necessary to develop better habits and using the list of skills obtained to suggest types of skills which a school might well develop in its students. Other investigations have been made of the values and ideals developed or cherished by adults under the assumption that an educational institution has as one of its duties helping to develop ideals and values in its students.

In addition to these studies of individual life some investigators have examined social groups to find out their practices, their problems, their concepts, ideas and their dominant values, to suggest group objectives of education. For example, in developing curricula for Indian schools studies have been made of each of a number of major tribes to find out characteristics of the tribes which would suggest needs and opportunities for education of the children in these Indian tribes. In similar fashion, investigations have been made of rural communities in contrast to city communities to identify problems and values and other data that would suggest educational objectives appropriate for these rural groups.

Studies have also been made of the factors conditioning life in particular communities or areas such as the natural

resources in the community, population changes, migra-
tion, direction of social change. These have been made on
the assumption that education should help a community
utilize most effectively its resources, to provide adequate
preparation for persons who are migrating as well as those
who are remaining within the community, to meet im-
minent social changes and the like. In all of these cases the
studies of contemporary life only give information about
the present status of the individual, the group, or the conditions of life within the community or region. They do
not directly give educational objectives. In order to suggest
objectives, the data from these studies must be interpreted,
that is, inferences have to be made from present status
regarding gaps, emphases and needs.

Perhaps the potential value of studies of contemporary
life can best be understood by collecting and analyzing
samples of data for yourself. I would suggest that you collect sample information of several sorts. On the one hand
it might be well to draw upon your memory, your experience in a given area of life such as in your civic life, to jot
down the activities that you engage in as a citizen. Also
list the problems that you have encountered as a citizen.
Imagine this information as being illustrative of what
might be obtained from a considerable sample of adults in
your community. In the light of such information, can you
suggest possible objectives which are implied by these
data?

Consider another kind of data which would also be
useful in this same area of civic life. Examine public opin-
ion polls over the last two or three years to identify the
areas in which citizens have little information and have
ineffective attitudes as a basis for their attack upon important social problems of today. Again, suggest what objectives are implied by the data obtained in this fashion.

Another illustration might be the examination of health

data within your community. Analyze the morbidity and the mortality statistics. Find out whether any public health surveys have been made in your area and any studies of nutritional status. With such data as you can obtain in this fashion, but taking at least six types of data, attempt to infer educational objectives and see what problems are involved in doing so.

The variety of ways by which information regarding activities, problems, and needs of contemporary life may be obtained is sometimes confusing. During the past twenty-five years hundreds of investigations have been made of contemporary life with a view to inferring educational objectives. These have involved observations of behavior, analyses of newspapers, of magazine articles, of the ideas of frontier thinkers about the important problems of the day, studies of community in sociological surveys as Lynds' volume on Middletown, or the Warner series on Yankee City, activity analyses of various kinds of individual activities as well as job analyses for a variety of vocations. Because the possible materials for analysis are so numerous and the possible methods of investigation are so varied, it becomes important to recognize again that analyses of contemporary life are possible at several levels. In the first place, some analyses of contemporary life are national in scope if not international, and do not need to be repeated by every school group working upon the curriculum. Data are already available to throw a good deal of light upon the possible objectives in the field of national and international affairs, data indicating critical social, political, and economic problems. There are also data in the general areas relating to music, the arts, and aesthetic life.

Some studies need to be made on a community-wide basis but do not need to be repeated for each school in the community. For example, some of the analyses of morbidity statistics and public health data can be done for the entire city or country without having to be repeated for each sub-community. On the other hand, there are types of information which must be obtained for the area served by a particular school and additional information that is necessary for a group of people within the school, as when one analyzes the health needs of the various ethnic or social groups within the community or school. Many of the public and private agencies of the community collect and record data of value in suggesting objectives.

Again, to get some conception of the way in which studies of this sort can be made and used, I would suggest taking a community with which you are very familiar and outlining the kinds of studies that are already available that would throw light upon the nature of contemporary life, then outline the sort of studies that would need to be made for the school as a whole to provide additional helpful information, and finally outline the particular kinds of information which an individual teacher or grade group would need to collect about community life. If possible, suggest the way in which the information might be obtained, and particularly consider kinds of interpretations that can be made of it. You will find the same problem of interpretation for data of this sort as you found in connection with interpretation of data about the learner. Any set of data permits multiple interpretation, and in many cases, a variety of data must be assembled in order to see some of the implications for educational objectives. I hope it will be possible for you to examine enough data to draw some interpretations about educational objectives from the data, and thus to see more clearly what the problems are and how the data may be used for suggesting objectives.

A good many courses have been built upon analyses made of life outside the school. The well-known Rugg series of social-studies books was developed from an analysis made of contemporary critical social problems as indicated by the studies made of so-called frontier thinkers, that is, leaders in the social science field. A number of the language art series of texts in use in the schools were made by making an analysis of the errors people of today commonly make in language usage. Some well-known texts in arithmetic have been built around a collection of the arithmetic problems with which adults are encountered. One of the early studies of this sort was carried on by G. M. Wilson when he was at Connersville, Indiana. He had students in the school obtain from their parents for several days the problems they were having to solve that involved arithmetic. The collection and analysis of this set of problems suggested the arithmetic operations and the kinds of mathematical problems which are commonly encountered by adults, and became the basis of an arithmetic curriculum.

Increasingly, the community schools in the South are basing much of their curriculum material upon analyses of community needs, with special reference to better utilization of natural resources, and more adequate development of human resources as revealed by community surveys. Studies of contemporary life provide a prolific source of information for suggestions regarding objectives.

Suggestions About Objectives from Subject Specialists

This is the source of objectives most commonly used in typical schools and colleges. School and college textbooks are usually written by subject specialists and largely reflect their views. Courses of study prepared by school and college groups are usually worked out by subject specialists and represent their conception of objectives that the school should attempt to attain. The reports of the Committee of Ten that appeared at the turn of the century had a most profound effect upon American secondary education for at least twenty-five years. Its reports were prepared by subject specialists and the objectives suggested by them were largely aimed at by thousands of secondary schools.

Many people have criticized the use of subject specialists on the grounds that the objectives they propose are too technical, too specialized, or in other ways are inappropriate for a large number of the school students. Probably the inadequacy of many previous lists of objectives suggested by subject specialists grows out of the fact that these specialists have not been asked the right questions. It seems quite clear that the Committee of Ten thought it was answering the question: What should be the elementary instruction for students who are later to carry on much more advanced work in the field? Hence, the report in History, for example, seems to present objectives for the beginning courses for persons who are training to be historians. Similarly the report in Mathematics outlines objectives for the beginning courses in the training of a mathematician. Apparently each committee viewed its job as outlining the elementary courses with the idea that these students taking these courses would go on for more and more advanced work, culminating in major specialization at the college or university level. This is obviously not the question that subject specialists should generally be asked regarding the secondary school curriculum. The question which they should be asked runs somewhat like this: What can your subject contribute to the education of young people who are not going to be specialists in your field; what can your subject contribute to the layman, the garden variety of citizen? If subject specialists can present answers to this question, they can make an important contribution, because, presumably, they have a considerable knowledge of the specialized field and many of them have had opportunity both to see what this subject has done for them and for those with whom they work. They ought to be able to suggest possible contributions, knowing the field as well as they do, that it might make to others in terms of its discipline, its content, and the like.

Some of the more recent curriculum reports do indicate that subject specialists can make helpful suggestions in answers to this question. The various reports published by the Commission on the Secondary School Curriculum of the Progressive Education Association beginning with "Science in General Education," including "Mathematics in General Education," "Social Studies in General Education," and other titles have been very useful and have thrown some light on the question, "What can this subject contribute to the education of young people who are not to specialize in it?" Other groups have recently prepared somewhat similar reports which also seem promising. Committee reports from the National Council of Mathematics Teachers, the National Council of English Teachers, the National Council of Social Studies Teachers, are cases in point. In general, they recognize much more clearly than did the committee preparing reports for the Committee of Ten that the subject is expected to make contributions to a range of students not considered in the earlier reports. In general, the more recent reports will be found useful as an additional source for suggestions about objectives.

Most of the reports of subject groups do not stop with objectives and many of them do not list objectives specifically. Most of them begin with some outline indicating their conception of the subject field itself and then move on to indicate ways in which it can be used for purposes of general education. Persons working on the curriculum will find it necessary to read the reports in some detail and at many places draw inferences from the statements regarding objectives implied. In general, two kinds of suggestions can be got from the reports as far as objectives are concerned. The first is a list of suggestions regarding the broad functions a particular subject can serve, the second is with regard to particular contributions the subject can make to other large functions which are not primarily functions of the subject concerned.

Let me illustrate these two types of suggestions that can be got from these reports. Recent reports of English groups, for example, have suggested educational functions of English as a study of language. The first function is to develop effective communication including both the communication of meaning and the communication of form. The second type of contribution is to effective expression, including in expression the effort of the individual to make internal adjustments to various types of internal and external pressures. A third function of language is to aid in the clarification of thought as is provided, for example, by the use of basic English as a means of aiding students to see whether they understand ideas clearly enough to translate them into operational words. This last function of clarification of thought is well illustrated by the statement of George Herbert Palmer that when confused he used to write himself clearheaded.

In the realm of literature these English committees see various kinds of contributions in terms of major functions literature can serve. Some emphasize its value in personal exploration. Literature in this sense can provide an opportunity for the individual to explore kinds of life and living far beyond his power immediately to participate in, and also give him a chance to explore vicariously kinds of situations which are too dangerous, too fraught with consequences for him to explore fully in reality. A number of committee reports speak of the general function of literature in providing greater extension to the experience of young people, not limited by geographic opportunities, nor limited in time nor limited in social class or types of occupations or social groups with which they can participate. In this case literature becomes the means of widely extending the horizon of the reader through vicarious experience. Another function of literature is to develop reading interests and habits that are satisfying and significant to the reader. Some English committees stress as an important objective to develop increasing skill in interpreting literary material, not only skill in analyzing the logical development and exposition of ideas but also the whole range of things including human motives which are formulated in written language and can therefore be subject to study and critical interpretation. Finally, some English committees propose that literature serves the function of appreciation, including both an opportunity for significant emotional reactions to literary forms and also opportunities for critical appraisal both of form and content, and a means thereby of developing standards of taste in literature.

These suggestions with regard to possible major functions of language and literature provide large headings under which to consider possible objectives which the school can aim at through language and literature. Such an analysis indicates the pervasive nature of the contribution that language and literature might possibly make to the development of children, adolescents, or adults. They suggest objectives that are more than knowledge, skills, and habits; they involve modes of thinking, or critical interpretation, emotional reactions, interests and the like.

Another illustration of the suggestions of major functions a subject may serve can be obtained from recent reports of science committees. One such report suggests three major functions science can serve for the garden variety of citizen. The first of these is to contribute to the improvement of health, both the individual's health and public health. This includes the development of health practices, of health attitudes, and of health knowledge, including an understanding of the way in which disease is spread and the precautions that can be taken by the community to protect itself from disease and from other aspects of poor health. The second suggested function of science is the use and conservation of natural resources; that is, science can contribute to an understanding of the resources of matter and energy that are available, the ways in which matter and energy can be obtained and utilized so as not greatly to deplete the total reserves, an understanding of the efficiency of various forms of energy transformation, and an understanding of plant and animal resources and the ways in which they can be effectively utilized. The third function of science is to provide a satisfying word-picture, to get clearer understanding of the world as it is viewed by the scientist and man's relation to it, and the place of the world in the larger universe. From these suggested functions of science, again it is possible to infer a good many important objectives in the science field, objectives relating to science, knowledge, attitudes, ability to solve problems, interests and the like.

Recent art reports illustrate another example of suggestions regarding major functions a subject might serve in general education. Some five functions have been proposed in these reports. The first, and in terms of Monroe's writing the most important, is the function of art in extending the range of perception of the student. Through art one is able to see things more clearly, to see them through the eyes of the artist, and thus to get a type of perception he is not likely to obtain in any other way. Both art production and art criticism are likely to extend perception. A second function proposed for art is the clarification of ideas and feelings through providing another medium for communication in addition to verbal media. There are students who find it possible to express themselves and communicate more effectively through art forms than through writing or speaking. For them this is an important educational function of art. A third function is personal integration. This refers to the contribution art has sometimes made to the relieving of tensions through symbolic expression. The making of objects in the studio and shop and expression through dancing and through music have long been known to produce an opportunity for personal expression and personal release from tension that is important in providing for the better integration of some young people. A fourth function is the development of interests and values. It is maintained that aesthetic values are important both as interesting qualities for the student and also as expressing very significant life values in the same category with the highest ultimate values of life. On this basis the contribution art can make in providing satisfaction of these interests and in developing an understanding of and desire to obtain these art values is an important educational function of art. Finally, a fifth function of art is the development of technical competence, a means of acquiring skill in painting or drawing or music, or some other art form which can have meaning and significance to the art student. These art reports are another illustration of material from which a number of significant suggestions regarding educational objectives can be inferred from a statement of functions.

A second type of suggestion that can be got from reports of subject specialists are the particular contributions that a subject can make to other large educational functions, that may not be thought of as unique functions of the subject itself. The Report of the Committee on Science in General Education is an excellent illustration of this type of suggestion. This report is organized in terms of suggested contributions science can make in each of the major areas of human relationships. In personal living, for example, suggestions are made as to ways in which science can help to contribute to personal health, to the need for self assurance, to a satisfying world picture, to a wide range of personal interests, and to aesthetic satisfaction. In the area of personal-social relations, suggestions are made as to ways in which science may help to meet student needs for increasingly mature relationships in home and family life and with adults outside the family, and for successful and increasingly mature relationships with age mates of both sexes. In the area of social-civic relations suggestions are made as to how science may help to meet needs for responsible participation in socially significant activities, and to acquire social recognition. In the area of economic relations suggestions are made as to how science may help to meet needs for emotional assurance of progress toward adult status, to meet the need for guidance in choosing an occupation and for vocational preparation, to meet the need for the wise selection and use of goods and services, and to meet the needs for effective action in solving basic economic problems.

The volume *Science in General Education* then goes on to outline the ways in which science can be taught to encourage reflective thinking and to develop other characteristics of personality such as creative thinking, aesthetic appreciation, tolerance, social sensitivity, self-direction. Critics have questioned the depths of contributions that science might make on a number of these points, but it is clear that these suggestions are useful in indicating possible objectives that a school might wish to aim at, using science or other fields as a means for attaining these objectives. Other subject groups have, in similar fashion, made suggestions regarding specific contributions these subjects might make to areas that are not uniquely the responsibility of these subjects. It is then through the drawing of inferences from reports of this sort regarding both the major functions that specialists think the subject can make and also the more specific contributions that the subject might make to other major functions that one is able to infer objectives from the reports of subject specialists.

I would suggest in order to get some taste of the kind of thing that can be obtained from these reports that you read at least one subject report at the level in which you are interested and jot down your interpretation of the major functions the committee believes that this subject can serve and the more specific contributions it can make to other educational functions. Then, formulate a list of the educational objectives you infer from these statements. This will give you some idea of the kinds of objectives that are likely to be suggested by the reports that are being made by various subject groups.

The Use of Philosophy in Selecting Objectives

The suggestions regarding objectives obtained from the three sources previously cited provide more than any school should attempt to incorporate in its educational program. Furthermore, some of these suggested objectives are inconsistent with others. A smaller number of consistent highly important objectives need to be selected. A small number rather than many should be aimed at since it requires time to attain educational objectives; that is, time is required to change the behavior patterns of human beings. An educational program is not effective if so much is attempted that little is accomplished. It is essential therefore to select the number of objectives that can actually be attained in significant degree in the time available, and that these be really important ones. Furthermore, this group of objectives should be highly consistent so that the student is not torn by contradictory patterns of human behavior.

To select a group of a few highly important, consistent objectives it is necessary to screen the heterogeneous collection of objectives thus far obtained so as to eliminate the unimportant and the contradictory ones. The educational and social philosophy to which the school is committed can serve as the first screen. The original list of objectives can be culled by identifying those that stand high in terms of values stated or implied in the school's philosophy.

Let me illustrate the way in which an educational and social philosophy can actually operate as a screen for selecting and eliminating educational objectives. An adequate formulation of an educational and social philosophy will include the answers to several important questions. In essence the statement of philosophy attempts to define the nature of a good life and a good society. One section of an educational philosophy would outline the values that are deemed essential to a satisfying and effective life. Quite commonly, educational philosophies in a democratic society are likely to emphasize strongly democratic values. For example, one such statement of philosophy emphasizes four democratic values as important to effective and satisfying personal and social life. These four values are (1) the recognition of the importance of every individual human being as a human being regardless of his race, national, social, or economic status; (2) opportunity for wide participation in all phases of activities in the social groups in the society; (3) encouragement of variability rather than demanding a single type of personality; (4) faith in intelligence as a method of dealing with important problems rather than depending upon the authority of an autocratic or aristocratic group.

When a school accepts these values as basic the implication is that these are values to be aimed at in the educational program of the school. They suggest educational objectives in the sense that they suggest the kinds of behavior patterns; that is, the types of values and ideals, the habits and practices which will be aimed at in the school program. Objectives that are consistent with these values will be included and suggested objectives which are inconsistent with these values will not be included in the school's educational program.

The school's philosophy will undoubtedly by implication deal with two other types of values widely acclaimed in contemporary life outside the school; namely, material values and success. Many schools are likely to state in their philosophy that they do not accept the contemporary emphasis on materialism and that they do not believe financial, personal or social success as usually defined are desirable educational values. Again, such a decision immediately has implications in the selection of educational objectives. Suggestions that are made implying that this or that skill or this or that habit or practice will contribute to material rewards or will make for this kind of success are likely to be eliminated, whereas objectives that lead toward spiritual values of the sort previously indicated will be given higher rank. In this way that section of the school's philosophy which formulates the values it holds high can be used directly as a means for selecting and eliminating educational objectives.

A statement of educational philosophy will also deal with the question, "Should the educated man adjust to society, should he accept the social order as it is, or should he attempt to improve the society in which he lives?" Another way of stating this question is in this form, "Should the school develop young people to fit into the present society as it is or does the school have a revolutionary mission to develop young people who will seek to improve the society?" Perhaps a modern school would include in its statement a position that has some of both of these implications; that is, it believes that the high ideals of a good society are not adequately realized in our present society and that through the education of young people it hopes to improve society at the same time that it helps young people to understand well enough and participate competently enough in the present society to be able to get along in it and to work effectively in it while they are working to improve it. However these questions may be answered, the answer in turn affects the educational objectives that are selected. If the school believes that its primary function is to teach people to adjust to society it will strongly emphasize obedience to the present authorities, loyalty to the present forms and traditions, skills in carrying on the present techniques of life; whereas if it emphasizes the revolutionary function of the school it will be more concerned with critical analysis, ability to meet new problems, independence and self-direction, freedom, and self-discipline. Again, it is clear that the nature of the philosophy of the school can affect the selection of educational objectives.

Another question with which the school's philosophy will need to deal can be stated, "Should there be a different education for different classes of society?" If the answer is "yes," then the practice of setting up different objectives for children of lower social classes who leave school early to go to work may be justified. On the other hand, if the answer to this question is "no," if the school believes in a common democratic education for all, then in place of having differentiated objectives for different classes of youngsters in the school an effort is made to select common objectives that are personally and socially significant and the school tries to develop ways of attaining these common objectives with a wide variety of types of young people. Closely allied to this question is another, "Should public school education be aimed primarily at the general education of the citizen, or should it be aimed at specific vocational preparation?" Again, the answer to this question clearly affects the kinds of objectives that are given greater emphasis and are selected for major attention in the school's program.

One more illustration may be enough to indicate the

kind of matters that are dealt with in a statement of the school's educational philosophy and how this statement can then be used in selecting educational objectives. Many schools, particularly after the outbreak of the War, formulated their educational philosophies in terms that were called democratic. They derived their conception of the good life for the individual and for the society in terms of an ideal democratic society. This immediately raises the question, "Is democracy to be defined solely in political terms, or does democracy imply a way of life at home, in the school, and in economic matters, as well as a form of political life." If the school's philosophy conceives democracy as a way of life appropriate for all phases of living, it then becomes necessary to give major emphasis to objectives that aim at the development of democratic values, attitudes, knowledges, skills, and abilities not only for a political democracy but for democracy in all of the aspects of life.

For a statement of philosophy to serve most helpfully as a set of standards or a screen in selecting objectives it needs to be stated clearly and for the main points the implications for educational objectives may need to be spelled out. Such a clear and analytical statement can then be used by examining every proposed objective and noting whether the objective is in harmony with one or more main points in the philosophy, is in opposition or is unrelated to any of these points. Those in harmony with the philosophy will be dentified as important objectives.

The Use of a Psychology of Learning in Selecting Objectives

There is a second screen through which the suggested objectives should be passed and that is the criteria for objectives implied by what is known about the psychology of learning. Educational objectives are educational ends, they are results to be achieved from learning. Unless these ends are in conformity with conditions intrinsic in learning they are worthless as educational goals.

At the lowest extreme a knowledge of the psychology of learning enables us to distinguish changes in human beings that can be expected to result from a learning process from those that can not. For example, it is quite clear that young people may develop health habits and health knowledge through a learning process, on the other hand they cannot increase their height directly by a learning process. Young children can learn to channel their physical reactions in more socially desirable directions as a matter of learning, but it is not possible through learning to inhibit physical reaction altogether. The old school of thought which attempted to teach children to be utterly quiet while they were in school was imposing an educational objective impossible of attainment.

At a higher level, a knowledge of the psychology of learning enables us to distinguish goals that are feasible from those that are likely to take a very long time or are almost impossible of attainment at the age level contemplated. For example, the personality structure of children is capable of a good deal of modification through educational experiences during the nursery and primary school period, but educational objectives which aim at profound changes in the personality structure of a sixteen-year-old are largely unattainable. At sixteen, so much of the development of the personality has already taken place that the re-education of basic personality structure is a very difficult task and unlikely to be attained through a normal school program.

Another use of knowledge of the psychology of learning is in connection with grade placement for objectives which are educationally attainable. Psychology of learning gives us some idea of the length of time required to attain an objective and the age levels at which the effort is most efficiently employed. When considering educational objectives for a range of grades, or age levels from this point of view, the process is termed, "grade-placement." However, relatively few studies in the psychology of learning definitively identify a single age level at which a given operation can be most efficiently learned. Hence, decisions on grade placement of particular objectives are more commonly aided by psychological knowledge regarding the sequence of learning that is implied for particular objectives. For example, it has been shown that in order to get effective learning in reading it is necessary for the child to have had concrete experiences to which are connected meaning vocabularies. Hence, preliminary experiences to build functioning vocabularies should precede intensive work in reading. Correspondingly, until a level of reading competence has been attained which includes a fairly well-mastered basic vocabulary it is useless to place much attention upon developing skills in careful and critical interpretation. Studies regarding the sequence of development are useful in deciding about the appropriateness of particular objectives at particular points in the sequence of the educational program.

Another type of judgment growing out of a study of psychology of learning has to do with the conditions requisite for the learning of certain types of objectives. One of the most useful is a group of studies that have been carried on regarding the forgetting of knowledge. In general, forgetting of knowledge learned is very rapid. One series of studies conducted at college level reported that 50 percent of the material known when the student finished a certain college course has been forgotten within one year and 80 percent had been forgotten in two years. These studies also suggest certain conditions that greatly reduce the forgetting of knowledge. One of these conditions is the opportunity to use this knowledge in daily life. This not only reduced the forgetting but it also increased the amount of knowledge the student acquired while taking the course. For example, in a study of a certain college science course it was shown that the knowledge that had direct application to the health and sanitary practices of the students was not so largely forgotten as was the knowledge not so readily applied—less than 15 percent compared to more than 50 percent in a year. This suggests that objectives concentrating on specific knowledge are more attainable and the results more permanent when there are opportunities for this knowledge to be used in the daily lives of the students.

Another illustration of the contribution of psychology of learning to conditions requisite for attaining given objectives can be given from studies of the time required to bring about certain types of changes in young people. It has been shown, for example, that to change the basic attitudes of children requires continuous emphasis extending over several years. In general, basic attitudes are not markedly shifted by one, two, three, or four months of instruction. In similar fashion data have been obtained regarding the time involved in bringing about other types of behavior changes, such as ways of thinking and study, basic habits and practices, interests, and the like. Obviously, psychological knowledge of this sort is useful in suggesting the length of time over which particular objectives will need to be emphasized.

One of the most important psychological findings for the curriculum maker is the discovery that most learning experiences produce multiple outcomes. For example, a youngster who is working upon arithmetic problems may be acquiring certain knowledge about the materials that are dealt with in arithmetic problems. For example, a recent study indicated that many persons thought that 6 percent compounded semiannually was the interest commonly to be expected on investments because many of the problems they had worked involved computations on the basis of 6 percent interest. Not only is the pupil gaining some knowledge of the materials about which the problems deal but he is also developing certain favorable or unfavorable attitudes toward arithmetic. He is developing or failing to develop certain interests in this area. In practically every educational experience two or more kinds of educational outcomes may be expected. This is important to the curriculum-maker because it suggests that greater efficiency of instruction is possible by capitalizing on the multiple results possible from each experience. The curriculum-maker should examine possible educational objectives to see how far several can be selected that can be developed together in the same experiences.

Another finding about learning conditions which has importance in selecting objectives is the evidence that learnings which are consistent with each other, which are in that sense integrated and coherent, reinforce each other; whereas learnings which are compartmentalized or are inconsistent with each other require greater time and may actually interfere with each other in learning. This suggests what may also be suggested by one's philosophy of education, that the various objectives be examined to see that they are mutually consistent and that they permit some degree of integration and coherent unification in the mind and action of the student so that the maximum psychological benefit of learning can thus be derived.

A psychology of learning not only includes specific and definite findings but it also involves a unified formulation of a theory of learning which helps to outline the nature of the learning process, how it takes place, under what conditions, what sort of mechanisms operate and the like. Since every teacher and curriculum-maker must operate on some kind of a theory of learning it is useful to have this theory of learning formulated in concrete terms both to check it for its tenability and also to see its implications for the curriculum. This theory of learning can have important implications for the nature of objectives. More than thirty years ago Professor Thorndike formulated a theory of learning which involved the idea that learning consisted of building up connections between specific stimuli and specific responses. Learning in these terms is a highly specific matter, similar to specific habit formation. Persons who hold such a theory as this must view objectives in highly specific terms. As a matter of fact, Professor Thorndike prepared two volumes on the psychology of mathematics—one on the psychology of algebra, the other on the psychology of arithmetic. In each of these volumes he formulated many hundreds of objectives. In arithmetic, for example, he stated more than 3,000 specific objectives for elementary school arithmetic on the ground that each different specific connection such as six plus three or three plus six had to be built up as a separate specific response to the specific stimulus. According to this theory then the kinds of objectives that need to be formulated are specific ones, very numerous and of the nature of specific habits.

On the other hand, Judd and Freeman at the University of Chicago at about the same time Thorndike was stating his theory, formulated a theory of learning called generalization which viewed learning as the development of generalized modes of attack upon problems, generalized modes of reaction to generalized types of situations. Judd and Freeman showed that many types of learning could be explained largely in terms of the learner's perceiving general principles that he might use or developing a general attitude towards the situation or method of attack which he could utilize in meeting new situations. If one holds to a generalized theory of learning, he then views objectives in more general terms, and he may talk about teaching youngsters to apply important scientific principles in explaining concrete phenomena, which would be viewed as one of the major generalized objectives for the science course. It is thus clear that one's theory of learning has considerable importance in determining how specifically objectives are to be stated and what kinds of statements can be viewed as educational objectives.

We have conducted a number of studies at the University of Chicago in connection with the learning of college students and our data in general are much more in harmony with the theory of generalization than they are with any theory of specific stimulus-response learning. Hence, I tend to view objectives as general modes of reaction to be developed rather than highly specific habits to be acquired. However, each curriculum-worker will need to formulate a theory of learning in which he has some confidence and use it as a basis for checking his educational objectives to see that they are consistent with his theory of learning.

To use a psychology of learning in selecting objectives it is helpful to write down the important elements of a defensible psychology of learning, and then to indicate in connection with each main point what possible implications it might have for educational objectives. Such a statement can then be used as a screen for proposed objectives. Possible objectives when checked against this statement may be selected as appropriate or may be rejected from a psychological viewpoint, because it is probably unattainable, inappropriate to the age level, too general or too specific, or otherwise in conflict with the psychology of learning.

Stating Objectives in a Form to be Helpful in Selecting Learning Experiences and in Guiding Teaching

As a result of the preceding steps the curriculum-maker has selected a small list of important objectives that are feasible of attainment. Because these objectives have been obtained from several sources they are likely to be stated in various ways. In organizing a single list of important objectives it is desirable to state these objectives in a form which makes them most helpful in selecting learning experiences and in guiding teaching.

Objectives are sometimes stated as things which the instructor is to do; as for example, to present the theory of evolution, to demonstrate the nature of inductive proof, to present the Romantic poets, to introduce four-part harmony. These statements may indicate what the instructor plans to do; but they are not really statements of educational ends. Since the real purpose of education is not to have the instructor perform certain activities but to bring about significant changes in the students' patterns of behavior, it becomes important to recognize that any statement of the objectives of the school should be a statement of changes to take place in students. Given such a statement, it is then possible to infer the kinds of activities which the instructor might carry on in an effort to attain the objectives—that is, in an effort to bring about the desired changes in the student. The difficulty of an objective stated in the form of activities to be carried on by the teacher lies in the fact that there is no way of judging whether these activities should really be carried on. They are not the ultimate purposes of the educational program and are not, therefore, really the objectives. Hence, although objectives are often stated in terms of activities to be carried on by the instructor, this formal statement operates as a kind of circular reasoning which does not provide a satisfactory guide to the further steps of selecting materials and devising teaching procedures for the curriculum.

A second form in which objectives are often stated is in listing topics, concepts, generalizations, or other elements of content that are to be dealt with in the course or courses. Thus, in an American history course, the objectives are sometimes stated by listing such headings as: the Colonial Period, the Establishment of the Constitution, the Westward Movement, the Civil War and Reconstruction, and Industrialization. Or, in a science class, the objectives are sometimes stated in the form of generalizations such as "Matter Can be Neither Created nor Destroyed," or "Green Plants Transform the Energy of the Sun into the Chemical Energy of Glucose." Objectives stated in the form of topics or generalizations or other content elements do indicate the areas of content to be dealt with by the students but they are not satisfactory objectives since they do not specify what the students are expected to do with these elements. In the case of generalizations, for example, is it expected that the student is to memorize these generalizations, or to be able to apply them to concrete illustrations in his daily life, or to view these generalizations as a kind of unified and coherent theory which helps to explain the nature of scientific explanation, or is there some other kind of use to which the student is expected to put these generalizations? In the case of a list of topics the desired changes in students are still more uncertain. If the history course is dealing with the Colonial Period what is the student expected to get from it? Are there certain facts about the period that he is to remember? Is he expected to identify trends in development that he can apply to other historic periods? Questions of this sort are not answered simply by stating objectives in terms of content headings or generalizations. The purpose of a statement of objectives is to indicate the kinds of changes in the student to be brought about so that the instructional activities can be planned and developed in a way likely to attain these objectives; that is, to bring about these changes in students. Hence, it is clear that a state-

ment of objectives in terms of content headings or generalizations is not a satisfactory basis for guiding the further
development of the curriculum.

A third way in which objectives are sometimes stated is
in the form of generalized patterns of behavior which fail
to indicate more specifically the area of life or the content
to which the behavior applies. For example, one may find
objectives stated as "To Develop Critical Thinking," "To
Develop Appreciation," "To Develop Social Attitudes,"
"To Develop Broad Interests." Objectives stated in this
form do indicate that education is expected to bring about
some changes in the students and they also indicate in
general the kinds of changes with which the educational
program is expected to deal. However, from what we know
about transfer of training it is very unlikely that efforts to
aim at objectives so highly generalized as this will be fruit-
ful. It is necessary to specify more definitely the content to
which this behavior applies, or the area in life in which such
behavior is to be used. It is not adequate to talk simply
about developing critical thinking without reference to the
content or the kinds of problems in which the thinking is to
be done. It is not a clear enough formulation of an objective to state that the aim is to develop wide interests without
specifying the areas in which the interests are to be aroused
and stimulated. It is not satisfactory to indicate that the
objective is to develop social attitudes without indicating
more clearly what the objects of the attitudes are that are
sought. Hence, the formulation of objectives in terms of
behavior types alone is not likely to prove a satisfactory
way of stating objectives if they are to be used as direct
guides to the further development of curriculum and instruction.

The most useful form for stating objectives is to express
them in terms which identify both the kind of behavior to be
developed in the student and the content or area of life in

which this behavior is to operate. If you consider a number of statements of objectives that seem to be clear and to provide guidance in the development of instructional programs, you will note that each of these statements really includes both the behavior and the content aspects of the objective.

Thus, the objective, "To Write Clear and Well-organized Reports of Social Studies Projects," includes both an indication of the kind of behavior—namely, writing clear and well-organized reports—and also indicates the areas of life with which the reports are to deal. Correspondingly, the objective, "Familiarity with Dependable Sources of Information on Questions Relating to Nutrition," includes both an indication of the sort of behavior, namely familiarity with dependable sources, and the content, namely, those sources that deal with problems of nutrition. As a third illustration of the way in which a clear objective includes both the behavioral and the content aspects, consider the objective, "To Develop an Appreciation of the Modern Novel." To develop appreciation implies a kind of behavior, although for many instructors it is necessary that this type of behavior be defined somewhat more clearly than is frequently done and the mention of the modern novel indicates the content to which the appreciation is to be applied. It can safely be concluded that a statement of objectives clear enough to be used in guiding the selection of learning experiences and in planning instruction will indicate both the kind of behavior to be developed in the student and the area of content or of life in which the behavior is to be applied.

Since a clearly formulated objective has the two dimensions of the behavioral aspect and the content aspect, it is often useful to employ a graphic two-dimensional chart to express objectives concisely and clearly. An illustration of such a chart is presented herewith. This is an illustration of the use of a two-dimensional chart in stating objectives for a high school course in biological science. It is not assumed that this course is an ideal course nor that these are ideal objectives. The purpose of the chart is to show how the chart can more compactly indicate the objectives that are being sought and how each objective is defined more clearly by the chart in terms both of the behavioral aspect and the content aspect.

Note that seven types of behavior are aimed at in this biological science course. The first type of behavior is to develop understanding of important facts and principles; the second type is to develop familiarity with dependable sources of information—that is, with places to which the student may go to get information likely to be dependable on questions of various sorts in the biological science field. The third type of behavior is to develop ability to interpret data—that is, to draw reasonable generalizations from the kinds of scientific data likely to arise in this field. The fourth type of behavior is to develop ability to apply principles that are taught in biological science to concrete biological problems that arise in his everyday life—hence, to be able to carry on problem-solving activities in this field. The fifth type of behavior is to develop the ability to study and report the results of study. The sixth is to develop broad and mature interests as they relate to biological science, and the seventh is to develop social rather than selfish attitudes in this area.

This statement of behavioral aspects should make clear that the biological science course aims at more than simply acquiring information. The specification of some seven kinds of behavior immediately suggests the need for learning experiences that will provide increased familiarity with sources of information, that will provide skill in interpreting data, skill in applying principles, practice in methods of study and reporting results of study, that will stimulate and challenge interests, that will develop attitudes favorable to the social uses of science and the like. Just a formulation of these behavioral headings does provide some leads as to the kind of curriculum planning that will be necessary.

However, the listing of the behavioral aspects is not a sufficient formulation of the objectives to be most useful. Hence, the chart also includes a statement of the content aspects of the objectives. It will be noted that the course is viewed as developing these various sorts of behavior in relation to the nutrition of human organisms, digestion, circulation, respiration, and reproduction. It is also noted that the course deals with the use of plant and animal resources so as to touch upon energy relationships, environmental factors conditioning plant and animal growth, heredity and genetics, and land utilization. Finally it is noted that the behavioral objectives relate to evolution and development. The formulation of the content aspects of the objectives have served still further to clarify the job to be done by the biological science course.

Finally, the chart indicates the relationship of these two aspects of the educational objectives. The intersections of the behavioral columns and the content rows are marked with X's when it is implied that the behavioral aspect applies to this particular area of content. Thus, for example, it may be noted that the student is expected to develop an understanding of important facts and principles in connection with every one of the content aspects. On the other hand, he is expected to develop familiarity with dependable sources of information only in connection with nutrition, reproduction, environmental factors conditioning plant and animal growth, heredity and genetics, land utilization, and evolution and development. The curriculum-maker planning this biological science course either foresaw little opportunity for emphasizing dependable sources of information in connection with other areas of content or decided

ILLUSTRATION OF THE USE OF A TWO-DIMENSIONAL CHART IN STATING OBJECTIVES FOR A HIGH SCHOOL COURSE IN BIOLOGICAL SCIENCE

Content Aspect of the Objectives	Behavioral Aspect of the Objectives						
	1. Understanding of important facts and principles	2. Familiarity with dependable sources of information	3. Ability to interpret data	4. Ability to apply principles	5. Ability to study and report results of study	6. Broad and mature interests	7. Social attitudes
A. Functions of Human Organisms							
1. Nutrition	X	X	X	X	X	X	X
2. Digestion	X		X	X	X	X	
3. Circulation	X		X	X	X	X	
4. Respiration	X		X	X	X	X	
5. Reproduction	X	X	X	X	X	X	X
B. Use of Plant and Animal Resources							
1. Energy relationships	X		X	X	X	X	X
2. Environmental factors conditioning plant and animal growth	X	X	X	X	X	X	X
3. Heredity and genetics	X	X	X	X	X	X	X
4. Land utilization	X	X	X	X	X	X	X
C. Evolution and Development	X	X	X		X	X	X

that the critical problems in the use of dependable sources were primarily in relation to the content areas indicated.

Correspondingly, ability to interpret data is defined as something to be developed in connection with each of the areas of content, whereas ability to apply principles is to be developed primarily in reference to all except evolution and development. Ability to study and present the results of study is a type of behavior which is to be developed in connection with all the areas of content included in the science course. In similar fashion it is expected that students will develop broad and mature interests in all the aspects of the course. Finally, it will be noted that social attitudes are to be developed particularly in relation to nutrition, reproduction, energy relationships, environmental factors conditioning plant and animal growth, heredity and genetics, land utilization, and evolution and development. It should be clear, therefore, that by the use of the X's it is possible concisely to indicate not only what kinds of behavior are to be developed in the biological science course but in connection with each of these kinds of behavior to show the particular areas of content or experiences to which the behavior is to apply.

When objectives are formulated on a two-dimensional chart of this sort it becomes a concise set of specifications to guide the further development of the course. For example, in the case of the illustrative chart, the instructor by looking at the several columns can see more clearly the kind of learning experiences that will have to be set up. It should be clear that the kind of experience the student needs to have in order to get understanding of important facts and principles is more than that required to memorize these things; it will involve analysis, interpretation, application to various illustrations to see the meaning; that is, it will involve the kind of mental operations that lead to a clearer interpretation and understanding. In similar fashion, the fact that the second column states familiarity with dependable sources of information provides a second specification. It is not enough that the student shall understand important facts and principles and remember them. He must also learn where to go to get dependable information as he needs it. This implies experience in consulting various sources of information, some practice in analyzing these sources to see where they are adequate and where they are unsatisfactory, the development of certain criteria by which to judge the dependability of a particular source of information. In brief, the development of the kind of objective implied by the second column requires somewhat different learning experiences than those implied by the first column.

Similarly, the objectives implied by the third column set up certain specifications regarding the learning experiences to be provided. If a student is to develop ability to interpret data he must have some opportunity to come in contact with data that are new to him and some practice in trying to interpret the data. Furthermore, he must develop certain principles of interpretation so as to avoid over-generalization and other common errors. The kind of learning experiences involved in interpreting new data differs somewhat from those kinds implied by the first two columns since it involves presenting new data to students, providing opportunities for interpretation, providing some chance to see where interpretations fall short, and developing certain criteria for interpretation. The fourth column, ability to apply principles, sets a further specification for the needed learning experiences. If the student is to learn to apply principles to concrete problems arising in his own experience, he must learn to deal with problems that are new in the sense that many of them have not been taken up in the course; for he must not simply memorize ready-made solutions. The learning experiences should bring out the ways in which the facts and principles can properly be applied and some of the difficulties involved in making applications. The solutions to the problems developed as a result of application should also be tested to see how adequately the applications have been made. The column thus provides added specifications for the kind of learning experiences that would need to be provided in this biological science course.

The fifth column, ability to study and report the results of study, suggests other specifications since it indicates that the student is expected to develop some skill in study on his own part and some skill in preparing oral or written reports on this study. This again demands that the instruction be of such nature that the student will have a chance to carry on significant study activities in the identified areas of biological science and that the course shall give him an opportunity to present reports of his study, presumably, both written and oral reports. This again sets specifications for the nature of the learning experiences to be set up and the methods of instruction to be used.

The sixth column, broad and mature interests, implies still further specifications for the learning experiences of the curriculum. It implies that it is not enough for the students to understand, to analyze, to interpret, to apply, but it is also hoped that they will find satisfactions in the things they are dealing with in this course so that interests will be developed, broader interests than they had when they came into the course and more mature interests. To provide experiences likely to increase interests usually involves finding out something about students' present interests so as to build upon them, and examining possible learning experiences in terms of how satisfying and interesting they are likely to be to the students so that further interests may be built up. Again it seems clear that the specification of this type of behavioral objective has its direct implications in the planning of the learning experiences.

Finally, the last column, social attitudes, also has direct implications in planning of the curriculum. The proposal that students shall develop attitudes of a social rather than a selfish sort in connection with these aspects of biological science implies that the students consider to some extent the social effects of various types of biological knowledge and development. It also implies that some effort will be made to help students see the connection between certain practices in biological science and their social implications, and the connection between certain proposed social actions and their consequences so that the students will not view science in a completely neutral fashion but will see it is a possible contributor to social welfare. It may also imply that the student is to develop the desire to aid those biological developments that do contribute to social welfare rather than viewing biological developments merely as contributions to personal satisfaction and personal benefit. These illustrations may suggest the way in which the behavorial aspects of the objectives provide a clearer specification of the kind of curriculum materials, learning experiences, and instructional procedures to be used.

Turning to the content aspects of the objectives, we can also see how they serve to specify more clearly the steps to be taken for the further development of the curriculum. The rows of the chart indicate the content headings to which the behavioral aspects apply; but they also indicate in connection with the behavorial aspects, the specifics to be developed under each heading. Thus, under nutrition, important facts and principles are to be identified, dependable sources of information are to be worked with, new nutrition data are to be presented to students for interpretation, problems involving the application of the important facts and principles are to be provided, interesting materials in nutrition are to be found, and the social implications of nutrition work are to be sought out. In similar fashion, each column indicates the kind of content analysis required. Hence, by putting these two aspects of objectives together, we get a clear enough specification to indicate on the one hand the kinds of behavior changes that are aimed at, and on the other hand to specify the particular materials, the particular ideas, the particular kinds of situations to be used in connection with each of these behavioral objectives. This provides a much more adequate specification of the educational objectives for a particular course or for a whole school than is normally available in the formulations to be found in courses of study and other curriculum reports.

Sometimes in the discussion of the use of a two-dimensional chart the question is raised as to whether the particular items entered in the chart are appropriate objectives. It should be recalled that this device is not primarily a device for determining whether an objective is an appropriate objective or not. The preceding steps should have identified objectives and screened them so that the objectives which are recorded on the chart are objectives that have already been through the screening process. In this sense the function of the chart is merely to provide a form to state objectives so that their meaning is clearer and the way in which they can be used in setting up learning experiences is more obvious than would be the case if they were stated in other forms. However, it is true that in any process of development there is value in shuttling back and forth from one step to a preceding and subsequent step in the process. Hence, it is sometimes true that by formulating the objectives in terms of such a chart as this, suggestions are obtained regarding additional objectives that were not previously identified. Thus the very existence of gaps in the chart where there are no X's suggests the possibility that an objective might be identified which would fill in the gap and put an X there. This will raise, in effect, the question,

"Is this gap an objective that ought to have been included?" For example, in the case of the illustrative chart the first gap is found under familiarity with dependable sources of information relating to digestion. It suggests the possibility of the objective "Familiarity with Dependable Sources of Information about Digestion." However, in this case the study of contemporary life had shown little need for keeping up with new information about digestion. The most critical problems in adult life and the most common problems of the students in using sources involve information about nutrition and reproduction rather than digestion, respiration, or circulation. It was because of these data that the instructor did not include the objective "Familiarity with Dependable Sources of Information about Digestion, Circulation, and Respiration." On the other hand, in developing this chart the instructor had found the suggestion of an objective relating to social attitudes in regard to energy relationships but did not find suggestions about social attitudes toward evolution and development. However, as he considered this possible objective carefully and checked it against his philosophy of education and what he knew about educational psychology, he decided that this was a desirable objective in terms of his philosophy and psychology and thus entered that in the chart even though it had not been identified earlier in the process of developing the objectives. The significance of this fact is that although the use of such a chart is primarily to develop a form in which objectives can be stated more helpfully, the chart may also serve to suggest some possible gaps in objectives that can be examined and screened by the same criteria as are used for the orginal set of objectives.

Another question which somtimes arises has to do with the degree of generality or specificity to be desired in these formulations both of the behavioral aspect of the objectives and of the content aspect. So far as the behavorial aspect of the objectives is concerned, the problem of generality and specificity is one of obtaining the level of generality desired and that is in harmony with what we know about the psychology of learning. Other things being equal more general objectives are desirable rather than less general objectives. However, to identify appropriate learning experiences it is helpful to differentiate rather clearly types of behavior which are quite different in their characteristics. Hence, one can sharply differentiate such a behavioral classification as the acquisition of facts which may be viewed primarily as memorization and the ability to apply principles to new problems which involves primarily the interpretation and use of facts and principles. On the other hand, some headings fall in between; for example, understanding important facts and principles implies memorization, one knows what they are and can state them, but it also implies more than sheer memorization; it implies some ability to indicate the meaning, some ability to suggest illustrations of these facts and principles, and, in a limited sense, some ability to apply them to other situations. It is clear that the formulation of categories of behavioral objectives is partly a matter of judgment, although some fairly clear differentiations can be made. It is also clear that an attempt to make a large number of differentiations fails both because many differentiations in behavior are hard to make and also because the development of a large number of categories of behavior results in the instructor being unable to keep in mind the different kinds of behavioral objectives to be sought so that eventually they do not operate as guiding objectives. On these grounds, therefore, a list of seven to fifteen categories of behavioral objectives is likely to be found more satisfactory than a much larger number or a smaller number. In the work of the Eight-Year Study where we had to categorize behavior in order to determine what was to be appraised, we utilized some ten categories. These were: the acquistion of information, the development of work habits and study skills, the development of effective ways of thinking, the development of social attitudes, the development of interests, the development of appreciations, the development of sensitivities, the development of personal social adjustment, the maintenance of physical health, the development of a philosophy of life. These are not ideal categories, but they represent a number sufficiently large to permit differentiation of the widely different categories and sufficiently small to be easily remembered and to serve as a guide in the work of instruction.

The content categories also involve the problem of generality of specificity. In general, it is desired to have a sufficient number of content categories to differentiate the important from the less important content. Thus, in the biological science illustration if only the three major content categories were used, namely functions of human organisms, use of plant and animal resources, and evolution and development, there would still be the possibility that a good many categories of dead wood might be included under those headings. For example, under the functions of human organisms it is possible to include such content headings as mechanical action, rest and recreation, skin and protection, categories that under other circumstances might have importance but in terms of the identified objectives of this course were deemed relatively unimportant and were not included. The same is true under the other headings. One function, therefore, of the subheadings is to indicate areas of content that are important and appropriate and others that are not. A second purpose is to put together areas that are reasonably homogeneous areas for sampling content specifics rather than to use areas which are heterogeneous and include quite different kinds of content. The number of content headings most likely to be satisfactory will vary somewhat with circumstances but in general a number between ten and thirty is more likely to be usable than a smaller or larger number.

A word of caution is necessary in using this chart to formulate objectives in two-dimensional form. Each of the terms used in the behavioral headings and in the content headings should have meaning so that they do not represent vague generalities which have no concrete significance to the curriculum-maker and thus cannot guide him in the next steps of curriculum development. In the case of objectives that are inferred from studies of the learner, and from studies of life outside the school, it is likely that the suggestions obtained in this way would have fairly concrete meaning because they were inductively formulated and were thus used to represent a variety of definite, specific materials which give meaning to the behavioral and content headings. However, the objectives suggested by subject specialists and the occasional one obtained by the kind of analysis and thinking involved in making this chart have not neccessarily been given concrete meaning through specific illustrations. In such cases the curriculum-maker will need to consider possible meanings of the suggestions, examining them in various contexts until he has satisfactorily defined them and can use them in the next steps of the curriculum development process.

As an example of terms likely to be used without having adequate meaning one might suggest such stated objectives as "critical thinking," "social attitudes," "appreciations," "sensitivities," "personal-social adjustment." These headings are frequently used to indicate types of behavior changes to be sought. They have been given concrete meaning by some persons but they are sometimes used by those who have not associated any concrete meaning with them. One can define an objective with sufficient clarity if he can describe or illustrate the kind of behavior the student is

expected to acquire so that one could recognize such behavior if he saw it. For example, take the term "critical
thinking." This in general probably implies some kind of
mental operation involving the relating of facts and ideas
in contrast to mere apprehension or memorization of them.
In a particular case, however, it is necessary to define
"critical thinking" further than this, to specify the behavior
somewhat more precisely. The secondary school teachers
working in the Eight-Year Study defined "critical thinking"
as they were using the term to include three sorts of mental
behavior. The first involved inductive thinking; that is,
the interpretation of data, the drawing of generalizations
from a collection of specific facts or items of data. The
second involved deductive thinking; the ability to begin
with certain general principles already taught and to apply
them to concrete cases which, although new to the students,
are appropriate illustrations of the operation of the principles. The third aspect of thinking identified by these
teachers was the logical aspect by which they meant the
ability of the student to make material purporting to be a
logical argument and analyze this argument so as to identify
the critical definitions, the basic assumptions, the chains of
syllogisms involved in it and detect any logical fallacies or
any inadequacies in the logical development of it. By defining critical thinking in this way the teachers gave meaning to a term which previously had been vague to them, and
thus provided a base for understanding what curriculum
implications there might be whenever such a term was set
up as the behavioral aspect of an educational objective.

In similar fashion the term "appreciation of literature"
was defined by a group of English teachers to represent
their meaning of the term as they used it in connection with
educational objectives. They distinguished appreciation of
literature from simply being interested in it or from skill in
interpreting it. In effect, they identified appreciation with

the kind of reaction a student made to literature which he was reading. They identified such kinds of reaction as the desire to read more of it, the effort to learn more about the material, the author of it, and the conditions under which it was written, the effort to express oneself creatively as stimulated by the reading material, identification with one or more characters in the literary selection, an attempt to apply the ideas developed in the literary selection to the student's own experiences, the development of critical standards by which he attempted to decide how good the material was or how poor it was, in what respects it was good, in what respects it was poor. Others may not wish to accept this particular definition of appreciation but it should be clear that this was what these teachers meant by appreciation and that the definition of a behavioral objective in this way gives it concrete meaning so that it can serve as a useful educational objective. No doubt you will want to define some of the terms you use if you find in examining them that their meaning is not clear or does not have enough concreteness to serve to guide in the further development of the curriculum.

It is not usually difficult to define the content headings of a set of objectives. The tendency to use vague and abstract terms for the content headings is less frequent than for the behavioral headings. In some cases it may be necessary to indicate sub-headings of contents so as to define the particular headings by specification. Thus in the illustrative chart it might be wise to define evolution and development a little more clearly by indicating some of the subtopics or in some other way defining how much is to be included and what aspects of evolution and development are implied by such a heading as this. In other cases it may be useful to define the content heading by listing the particular problems, the particular generalizations, the particular situations in which the behavior is expected to operate so that there will be no misunderstanding and no inclusion of dead wood by failure to specify narrowly enough or concretely enough such a content heading included.

Perhaps these illustrations have been sufficient to indicate the problems involved in formulating objectives in a way that they can serve as useful guides in the further development of the curriculum. It should be clear that a satisfactory formulation of objectives which indicates both the behavioral aspects and the content aspects provides clear specifications to indicate just what the educational job is. By defining these desired educational results as clearly as possible the curriculum-maker has the most useful set of criteria for selecting content, for suggesting learning activities, for deciding on the kind of teaching procedures to follow, in fact to carry on all the further steps of curriculum planning. We are devoting much time to the setting up and formulation of objectives because they are the most critical criteria for guiding all the other activities of the curriculum-maker.

2

HOW CAN LEARNING EXPERIENCES BE SELECTED WHICH ARE LIKELY TO BE USEFUL IN ATTAINING THESE OBJECTIVES?

Thus far we have been considering the ends to be attained by the educational program. These ends or objectives have been defined in terms of the kind of behavior involved and the content with which the behavior deals. We next are to consider the question of how these ends can be attained. Essentially, learning takes place through the experiences which the learner has; that is, through the reactions he makes to the environment in which he is placed. Hence, the means of education are educational experiences that are had by the learner. In planning an educational program to attain given objectives we face the question of deciding on the particular educational experiences to be provided, since it is through these experiences that learning will take place and educational objectives will be attained.

Meaning of the Term "Learning Experience"

The term "learning experience" is not the same as the content with which a course deals nor the activities performed by the teacher. The term "learning experience" refers to the interaction between the learner and the external conditions in the environment to which he can react. Learning takes place through the active behavior of the student; it is what *he* does that he learns, not what the teacher does. It is possible for two students to be in the same class and for them to be having two different experiences. Suppose that the teacher is making an explanation and that one student is much interested in the problem and is following the explanation mentally, seeing the connections that are made and taking from his own experience certain

63

illustrations as the teacher goes along with the explanation. On the other hand, it is possible for the second student to be engrossed in thoughts of a forthcoming basketball game and to be devoting his attention entirely to planning for this game. It is obvious that although the students are in the same class, they are not having the same experience. The essential means of education are the experiences provided, not the things to which the student is exposed.

This definition of experience as involving the interaction of the student and his environment implies that the student is an active participant, that some features of his environment attract his attention and it is to these that he reacts. The question may be raised as to how far it is possible for a teacher to provide an educational experience for a student since the student himself must carry on the action which is basic to the experience. The teacher can provide an educational experience through setting up an environment and structuring the situation so as to stimulate the desired type of reaction. This means that the teacher must have some understanding of the kinds of interests and background the students have so that he can make some prediction as to the likelihood that a given situation will bring about a reaction from the student; and, furthermore, will bring about the kind of reaction which is essential to the learning desired. This theory of learning does not lessen the teacher's responsibility because it recognizes that it is the reactions of the learner himself that determine what is learned. But it does mean that the teacher's method of controlling the learning experience is through the manipulation of the environment in such a way as to set up stimulating situations—situations that will evoke the kind of behavior desired.

It should also be noted that it is possible for each student in the class to have a different experience even though the external conditions appear to be the same. This places considerable responsibility upon the teacher, both to set up situations that have so many facets that they are likely to evoke the desired experience from all the students or else the teacher will vary the experiences so as to provide some that are likely to be significant to each of the students in the class. The problem, then, of selecting learning experiences is the problem of determining the kinds of experience likely to produce given educational objectives and also the problem of how to set up situations which will evoke or provide within the students the kinds of learning experiences desired.

General Principles in Selecting Learning Experiences

Although the particular learning experiences appropriate for attaining objectives will vary with the kind of objectives aimed at, there are certain general principles that apply to the selection of learning experiences, whatever the objectives may be. The first of these is that for a given objective to be attained, a student must have experiences that give him an opportunity to practice the kind of behavior implied by the objective. That is to say, if one of the objectives is to develop skill in problem solving, this cannot be attained unless the learning experiences give the student ample opportunity to solve problems. Correspondingly, if another objective is to develop interest in reading a wide variety of books, this objective cannot be attained unless the student has opportunity to read a wide variety of books in a way that gives him satisfaction. This is true in connection with every type of objective, that it is essential that learning experiences be set up which give an opportunity for the student to practice the kind of behavior implied by the learning experience.

Since the complete definition of the objective includes not only a statement of the kind of behavior involved, but also a statement of the kind of content with which the behavior deals, it is also true that the learning experiences must give the student opportunity to deal with the kind of content implied by the objective. Hence, if the objective includes the ability to solve problems of health, it is necessary that the learning experiences give the student opportunity not only to solve problems but to work particularly upon health problems. If the objective in relation to interests is to develop interest in reading a wide variety of novels, then it is important that the learning experience not only give opportunity for reading but also for reading various sorts of novels. This is a basic principle useful in selecting learning experiences for all types of objectives.

A second general principle is that the learning experiences must be such that the student obtains satisfactions from carrying on the kind of behavior implied by the objectives. For example, in the case of learning experiences to develop skill in solving health problems, it is important that the experience not only give the student an opportunity to solve health problems, but also that effective solutions to these problems shall be satisfying to him. If the experiences are unsatisfying or distasteful, the desired learning is not likely to take place. In fact, it is more likely that he will develop the opposite from the desired objective. The same thing is true in the case of learning experiences to develop reading interests. The experiences must not only give him a chance to do this wide reading, but there must be satisfactions obtained from this kind of behavior in order for the learning experience to be effective. This requires the teacher to have sufficient information about the students' interests and needs and about basic human satisfactions to judge whether or not given learning experiences are likely to prove satisfying to the students involved.

A third general principle with regard to learning experiences is that the reactions desired in the experience are within the range of possibility for the students involved. That is to say, the experiences should be appropriate to the student's present attainments, his predispositions, and the like. This is another way of stating the old adage that "the teacher must begin where the student is." If the learning experience involves the kind of behavior which the student is not yet able to make, then it fails in its purpose. This too requires the teacher to have sufficient information about his students to know whether their present attainments, their present background, and their present mental sets are such that the desired behavior is possible for them.

A fourth general principle is that there are many particular experiences that can be used to attain the same educational objectives. As long as the educational experiences meet the various criteria for effective learning, they are useful in attaining the desired objectives. There are probably an uncertain number of experiences that could be thought of and worked out to attain particular objectives. This means that the teacher has a wide range of creative possibility in planning particular work. This also means that it is possible that a given school may develop a wide range of educational experiences all aiming at the same objectives but capitalizing on the various interests of both students and faculty members. It is not necessary that the curriculum provide for a certain limited or prescribed set of learning experiences in order to assure that the desired objectives are attained.

A fifth principle is that the same learning experience will usually bring about several outcomes. Thus, for example, while the student is solving problems about health, he is also acquiring certain information in the health field. He is also likely to be developing certain attitudes toward the importance of public health procedures. He may be developing an interest or a dislike for work in the field of health. Every experience is likely to bring about more than one learning objective. On the positive side this is a decided advantage because it permits economy of time. A well-planned set of learning experiences will be made up of experiences that at the same time are useful in attaining several objectives. Negatively, it means that the teacher must always be on the lookout for undesirable outcomes that may develop from a learning experience planned for some other purpose. Thus, the effort of the teacher to develop skill in interpreting Shakespeare's plays may be pushed to a point that at the same time the student is developing a strong dislike for Shakespeare. Or, the teacher who chooses arithmetic problems only to a view to the opportunity it provides for the practice in mathematical computation may inadvertently choose content which gives students the wrong idea about the particular phase of life with which the problems deal.

Illustrations of the Characteristics of Learning Experiences Useful in Attaining Various Types of Objectives

Since the number of possible objectives is very large, it is not possible to include a comprehensive statement of the characteristics of learning experiences useful for attaining every type of objective. Instead, we shall consider a sample of common types of objectives, noting some of the important characteristics required of effective learning experiences to attain these objectives.

1. *Learning experiences to develop skill in thinking.* The term "thinking" is used in a variety of ways, but, in general, the kind of behavior implied is the relating of two or more ideas rather than simply remembering and repeating these ideas. Inductive thinking involves drawing generalizations from several items of specific data. Deductive thinking involves applying one or more generalizations to specific cases.

Logical thinking involves the arrangement of assumptions, premises, and conclusions in a way to develop a logical argument. Quite commonly, in particular situations, several kinds of thinking will be required so that it is rare for a teacher to concentrate upon only one aspect of thinking. Since the learning experience must give the student opportunity to do these kinds of thinking, it is important that the situation be such as to stimulate this kind of behavior. Studies of learning in this field indicate that as students are faced with problems which they cannot answer immediately, it is more likely that they will be led to various types of thinking. This means that learning experiences to develop thinking will utilize various problems—problems that are real to students so as to stimulate their reaction. Furthermore, the problems should not be the kinds of questions in which the answers can be immediately obtained by looking them up in the textbook or some other reference material. The problems should be of the sort that require the relating of various facts and ideas in order to get any kind of solution. It is also desirable that the problems be set up in the kind of environment in which such problems usually arise in life. This is more likely to result in his viewing this as a real problem worthy of his effort to solve.

As the student is getting initial experience in solving problems, it will be necessary to set the situation so that he will see and follow the steps of thinking in their normal sequence. This may include such steps as (a) sensing a difficulty or a question that cannot be answered at present, (b) identifying the problem more clearly by analysis, (c) collecting relevant facts, (d) formulating possible hypotheses, that is, possible explanations or alternative solutions to the problem, (e) testing the hypotheses by appropriate means, and (f) drawing conclusions—that is, solving the problem. In formulating possible hypotheses, he will frequently be able to draw upon generalizations or principles that he already knows and may in this case be able to solve the problem immediately without testing the hypothesis that this principle is relevant. In particular cases, these steps in problem solving may vary and certain of them may not be necessary; but, in general, the learning experiences should give the student an opportunity to follow through the essential steps in problem solving to see what each of the steps involves and to become skillful in taking the necessary steps.

It should, of course, be obvious that the student learns to think through the experience of solving problems for himself. He has not acquired the objective when the teacher does the problem solving and the student only watches. It should also be evident that certain of the steps of problem solving are likely to require attention at different stages in the student's maturity. For example, the step involving the collection of relevant facts in order to have a basis for suggesting possible solutions requires a special practice in the earlier years of the elementary and secondary school. Unfortunately, in mathematics the student usually is given all the facts he needs so that all he has to do is make the computation. Later, when he is faced with the necessity of getting certain of the facts for himself, he is frequently at a loss to know what facts he needs and where they can be found. Experiments have shown that students who are given special practice in deciding on relevant facts needed and where and how to get them showed greater improvement in learning to solve problems. On the other hand, emphasis upon ways of collecting relevant facts may not be so essential in the college and graduate school if the students have already acquired skill in this process in their earlier education.

Some learning experiments have been conducted in seeking to answer the question, "Does it help to teach students to use a set form in analyzing a problem?" One investigation was made with children in the ninth grade. It was found that the pupils used several different ways in attacking the problems. They found that some students could see ahead and eliminate some of the intermediate steps in problem solving. Others would have to go through a detailed routine laboriously step by step through each phase of the analysis. When all the students were taught one particular method of analysis, it was found that the slower students improved appreciably, but this method of teaching was of no particular benefit to the brighter students. It suggests that some students must be taught step by step to analyze a problem while others are often able to make large mental jumps and do not have to be given a detailed form of analysis.

Another point which is often difficult for students is to outline possible solutions or explanations. Most students, unless they are unusually fertile, are not able to suggest more than one or two solutions or explanations. There is evidence to show that help given at this point in learning is productive of improved problem solving. It is helpful to show students a number of solutions or a number of possible facts and conditions that have to be considered and to have them practice suggesting various possibilities when they are attacking problems.

Another point of difficulty in problem solving is the lack on the part of some students of a concept structure by which to analyze the problem and to deal with the various elements in it. Teaching students to think includes giving them practice in using basic concepts and schemes of viewing the particular phenomenon about which the thinking is going on so that they have the mechanism by which to analyze and to deal with the problem. This is the real function of technical terms in some fields, the basic assumptions and generalizations. They serve to provide a kind of concept structure by which a student is able to consider the problem and to relate the various elements of the phenomenon involved. Frequently, particular experiences related to the use of such a concept structure may be necessary in providing the basis for effective problem solving.

2. *Learning experiences helpful in acquiring informa-tion.* This type of learning experience includes such objectives as developing understanding of particular things, developing knowledge about various things, and the like. Usually, the kind of information to be acquired includes principles, laws, theories, experiments and the evidence supporting generalizations, ideas, facts, and terms. It is assumed that such an objective is important only if the information is viewed as functional; that is, being useful in connection with the student's attack upon problems or with the guidance of his practices and the like. It is not assumed that information is of value as an end in itself.

It may be useful to examine some of the studies that throw light upon the inadequacy of present learning experiences for teaching information. Some five defects in the learning of information are commonly identified. The first of these is that students frequently memorize by rote rather than acquiring any real understanding or ability to apply the ideas which they remember. For example, John Dewey reports visiting a class in the vicinity of Chicago which was studying the way in which the earth was probably formed. Mr. Dewey asked the students whether, if they were able to dig down to the center of the earth, they would find it hot or cold there. No child could answer. The teacher then said to Mr. Dewey that he had asked the wrong question. She turned to the children and said, "Children, what is the condition at the center of the earth?" The children all replied in chorus, "In a state of igneous fusion." This memorization without understanding is altogether too common an effect of present experiences used to develop information. A second defect in the learning of information is revealed by the fact that many students show a very rapid rate of forgetting. In fact, most forgetting curves for specific information look very much like the forgetting curves for nonsense syllables first published by Meumann in the last century. Typically, students will have forgotten 50 percent of the information they acquire within a year after completing a course, and 75 percent within two years after completing a course.

A third defect is the lack of adequate organization. Many students remember information only as isolated bits and are unable to relate these items in any organized or systematic fashion. A fourth defect is the degree of vagueness and the large number of inaccuracies in what students recall. The more precise the information is, the less likely students will be to remember it or else they will remember it with large percentage of inaccuracy. Finally, students show very limited familiarity with sources of accurate and recent information. Since much information required for dealing with contemporary problems is information which needs to be kept up to date, it is very important for students to know where to turn to get accurate and dependable information. Yet, recent studies have shown that not more than 20 percent of the students are able to identify dependable sources of information in questions which they have been studying in school.

There are several suggestions that can be followed in setting up learning experiences to overcome these defects in the acquisition of information. In the first place, it has been shown that information can be acquired at the same time that students are learning to solve problems. Hence, it is more economical to set up learning situations in which the information is obtained as a part of a total process of problem solving than it is to set up special learning experiences just to memorize information. Furthermore, when information is acquired as a part of problem solving, the use of the information and the reasons for obtaining it are clear. This is less likely to result in rote memorization.

A second suggestion is to select only important information to include as worthy of remembering. In place of having thousands of technical terms to be learned, as is sometimes done in science courses, the number of terms selected should be much fewer and of sufficient importance and frequency of use that it will be possible for the students to acquire this information with accuracy and precision. There is much less likelihood of forgetting if the material is frequently used.

A third suggestion is to set up situations in which the intensity of impression and the variety of impressions of the information will increase the likelihood of remembering these important items. This means that items important enough to be remembered will be brought up in various ways and with a considerable degree of intensity rather than having them considered in an offhand fashion.

A fourth suggestion is to use these important items of information frequently and in varied contexts. The use of information frequently increases the probability of remembering it and by bringing it up in varied contexts, it increases the probability of later association and also gives more significance to the information dealt with.

In helping students to organize information they acquire, it is important that they do not conceive of the information in one scheme of organization alone. One is able to organize as he sees two or more ways in which the same material can be organized for effective use. This suggests that the learning situations will involve reorganization of information in varied ways appropriate to the different kinds of situations in which the information can be used.

So far as the development of familiarity with sources is concerned, it is necessary that students have practice in consulting sources and learn where dependable information of a given sort can be found. This can easily be provided in connection with learning experiences involving problem solving. It is much better to consult various sources to get dependable information than to depend solely upon a single text or a few references for this information.

It should be clear that the suggestion is that information be developed in these learning experiences when information is a part of something else, particularly problem solving, and that it is not desirable to set up learning experiences solely to memorize material.

3. Learning experiences helpful in developing social attitudes. Objectives that can be classified as developing social attitudes include those emphasized in the social studies, in literature, in the arts, physical education, extracurricular activities, and the like. Attitudes are defined as a tendency to react even though the reaction does not actually take place. Everyone has experienced a desire to do something, a feeling of readiness to react in a given way, which may precede overt reaction, and in some cases may be inhibited so that no overt reaction actually takes place. Thus, one may have an attitude of disgust toward a colleague but will not express it by verbal or physical means. The importance of attitudes arises from the fact that attitudes are strong influences upon behavior—that is, overt action—and also strongly influence the kinds of satisfactions and values which the individual chooses.

Studies of attitude development indicate that there are four chief means by which attitudes commonly develop in people. The most frequent method is through assimilation from the environment. The things that are taken for granted by the people round about us, the points of view that are commonly held by our friends and acquaintances are illustrations of environmental attitudes which are frequently assimilated without our having been conscious of them. A second and perhaps the next most common method of acquiring attitudes arises from the emotional effects of certain kinds of experiences. In general, if one has had satisfying experiences in a particular connection, he develops an attitude favorable to some content or aspect of that experience, while if he has had an unsatisfying effect from the experience, his attitude may become antagonistic. The third most frequent method of developing attitudes is through traumatic experiences, that is, experiences which have had a deep emotional effect. Thus, a youngster may develop overnight a great fear of dogs from one experience in having been bitten by a dog. Finally, a fourth method of developing attitudes is through direct intellectual processes. In some cases when we see the implications of particular behavior, when we analyze the nature of a particular object or process, we are led to develop an attitude favorable or unfavorable to it from the knowledge which we gain from this intellectual analysis. Unfortunately, attitudes formed through definite intellectual processes are not so frequent as those obtained in the other ways. Of these four methods of developing attitudes, the third is not likely to be useful to the school. Traumatic experiences involving the intense emotional reactions are too hard to control to be used systematically in an educational program. Hence, schools will have to lean heavily upon the use of a process of assimilation from the environment, of developing attitudes through emotional effects of particular experiences, and through direct intellectual processes.

Several generalizations may be suggested regarding learning experiences for developing attitudes. In the first place, the school and community environment should, so far as possible, be modified and controlled so as to promote desirable attitudes. In many modern communities there is disjunction between the school and the home, the school and the church, the school and the rest of the community with regard to the attitudes that are developed. The environments are inconsistent; values, points of view are taken for granted in the press that are denounced in the pulpit, the values emphasized in the motion pictures are in conflict with those which the school seeks to develop. There is a great need for seeking to modify the environment of the youngster throughout his experience in order to help him develop desirable social attitudes. This means increasing the degree of consistency of the environment and helping to reinforce the emphasis upon social rather than selfish attitudes.

It is particularly possible for the school to develop a more unified school environment in order to develop attitudes. If the faculty examines the things that are taken for granted in the points of view of staff members, in the rules and regulations and practices of the school, it is often possible to modify those markedly so as to develop a more unified environment that will help to emphasize social attitudes.

One common tendency in certain communities has tended to break down rather than to develop social attitudes: that is, a failure to consider the nature of the social structure existing outside the school and the assumption that the points of view of the middle class old American teachers were the desirable points of view even though they may be sharply in conflict with the social environment provided by various family and ethnic groups, and social class groups in the community. By strengthening the positive social attitudes in the community and making the school consistent with them rather than arbitrarily enforcing a particular set of views held by a given group of teachers, it is often possible to get a much greater degree of unity in the environment of children and hence to increase the development of social attitudes with them.

A second weakness to be overcome in many schools is the existence of antisocial conditions in the school. The acceptance of certain cliques, the intensification of social class lines within the school through the informal social organization and through the treatment the teachers give the different types of children may often develop selfish attitudes

without our having been conscious of it. A careful examination of the school environment will suggest many possibilities for using it to develop desirable attitudes.

In developing attitudes through the use of experiences
which have satisfying emotional concomitants, it is important to provide opportunity for the student to behave in the
way desired and to get satisfaction from it. For example, if
in the elementary school an effort is made to develop better,
more social attitudes toward other racial groups, it is important to provide experiences in which children have a chance
to share with children of other racial groups, to serve and to
be served by them, but in situations that give a good deal of
satisfaction from this type of sharing, this give and take. If
the children have planned a party together and have the
satisfaction from getting the thing carried through successfully, that is one illustration of setting up an experience in
which he desired social attitudes can be reflected and satisfactions can be obtained at the same time.

In using intellectual processes to develop social attitudes,
the experiences should be such as to provide a broad analysis of social situations, to develop, first, understanding and
then the desirable attitudes. In some cases, a frontal attack
upon some kinds of social problems is not possible. If the
students have prejudices and stereotyped conceptions, these
may inhibit their understanding and they fail to see the
logic of the social view. In this connection, it is often useful
to give students a chance to get first-hand experience with
the problem, to see for themselves the serious nature of
unemployment, for example, in order to get a sincere hear-
ing for possible ways of dealing with such a problem. Literature or motion pictures may often give a personal view of
some kind of social situation that would not be gained by
sheer study of the data alone. By the use of these methods,
problem areas can be opened up for study. Then when there
is clear understanding of the situation, it is possible to help

students to develop attitudes as they see the implications of the points of view they hold. Finally, in such a program of developing attitudes through intellectual processes, it is desirable periodically for students to review their conduct in a particular area, to help to check with the goals to which they give lip service, to see how far their own behavior is in harmony with what they profess to believe. This kind of periodic review helps also to influence and develop attitudes.

It should be clear that there is no way by which persons can be forced to have different attitudes. Shifts in attitudes grow out of the student's change in view and this comes from either a new insight and new knowledge about the situation or from the satisfaction or dissatisfaction he has obtained from particular views previously held or a combination of these procedures. Learning experiences, then, are set up so as to provide these kinds of opportunities for insight and for satisfactions.

4. Learning experiences helpful in developing interests.

Interests are of concern in education both as ends and means; that is, as objectives and as motivating forces in connection with experiences to attain objectives. At this point, however, we are considering interests as a type of objective. Interests are often emphasized as important educational objectives because what one is interested in largely determines what he attends to and frequently what he does. Hence, interests tend to focus behavior in particular directions rather than in others and as such are powerful determiners of the kind of person anyone is.

The basic requirement of learning experiences designed to develop interests is that they enable the student to derive satisfactions from the area of experience in which the interest is to be developed. Hence, learning experiences to develop interests should give students an opportunity to explore the areas in which interests are to be developed and to have satisfying results from these explorations. Satisfactions may grow out of several sources. There are so-called fundamental satisfactions which seem to be basic to all people. These include such things as the satisfaction from social approval; the satisfaction from meeting physical needs such as food, rest, and the like; satisfactions from success, that is, achieving one's aspirations and so on. Wherever possible, then, learning experiences which provide a chance for the student to obtain these fundamental satisfactions are also likely to develop interests in these activities.

A second basis upon which an activity can be satisfying is to have it linked with some other experience which is satisfying. The use of emotionally charged symbols, the setting of an individual activity in the context of a social activity are illustrations of trying to link a particular activity which is not in itself fundamentally satisfying with something which is satisfying so that the emotional effect will carry over and develop satisfaction in the thing that is linked with it. Hence, youngsters who do not get fundamental satisfactions from reading, for example, may be led to enjoy reading through setting it in a social situation which is satisfying or in connecting the reading with other enjoyable experiences.

With younger children who are in good health, the need for activity can largely be counted on to support the satisfaction in wide explorations of various kinds of activity. Until their interests have been narrowed and channeled, they are likely to get satisfaction from sheer sensations and from variety of free activity. Satisfaction of curiosity is also satisfying for young children. Hence, it is possible in working with younger age groups to count much more heavily upon sheer exploration as providing the basis for increased satisfaction as long as the exploration does not negate fundamental satisfactions as, for example, giving the student a sense of failure or being laughed at, or in other ways making the activity distasteful because it gives him negative results.

The most difficult problem is setting up learning experiences to try to make interesting a type of activity which has become boring or distasteful to the student. Such an activity does not become interesting through sheer repetition. It is necessary to use a new approach in order to shift interest. The new approach may involve using totally different materials or it may involve putting the learning experience in a totally new context which is enjoyable to the student.

Perhaps these four illustrations are enough to suggest the way in which one can work out a list of characteristics relating to the learning experiences that can be used in connection with each major kind of objective. In curriculum planning this kind of analysis should be made for each type of behavioral objective. Such an analysis will help to clarify further the definitions of behavior and will help greatly in the selection of learning experiences.

The fact that there are many learning experiences which can be used to attain a given objective and that the same experience can often be used to attain several objectives means that the process of planning learning experiences is not a mechanical method of setting down definitely prescribed experiences for each particular objective. Rather, the process is a more creative one; as the teacher considers the desired objectives and reflects upon the kinds of experiences that can occur to him or that he has heard others are using, he begins to form in his mind a series of possibilities of things that might be done, activities that might be carried on, materials that might be used. As these take shape, it would be well to write them down as possible learning experiences. As they are written down, they might be outlined in more detail to indicate what they would include. Such a tentative draft of certain learning experiences should then be checked carefully against the desired objectives to see first whether or not the proposed experiences give an opportunity for the student to carry on the kind of behavior implied by the objectives and also whether the experiences sample the kind of content implied by the objectives. Next, the proposed learning experiences can be checked by the criterion of effect. Will the experiences suggested likely be satisfying to the particular student for which they are planned? If they do not result in satisfying effects, they are not likely to bring about the results desired. Third, the proposed learning experiences can be checked in terms of readiness. Do they require actions that the students are not yet ready or able to perform? Do they run counter to certain prejudices or mind sets of the students? Finally, they can be checked for economy of operation. Does the experience provide for the attainment of several objectives or does it care for only one or two? Having checked the learning experiences by these general criteria, it may be well then to check them also against some of the more particular characteristics implied by the generalizations about characteristics of learning experiences required for different types of objectives. If the tentative formulation of experiences meets these criteria satisfactorily, then it would appear to be a promising plan to develop. If some of the criteria are not well met, there may be the possibility of revision in order to make the experiences more effective. If the experiences are largely inadequate in terms of these criteria, then the tentative formulation should be dropped and others developed. In this way the process of selecting learning experiences provides opportunity for creative proposals which are then carefully checked in terms of appropriate criteria. As a result, there is opportunity both for artistry and for careful evaluation in advance of setting up the definite plans for the instructional program.

3

HOW CAN LEARNING EXPERIENCES BE ORGANIZED FOR EFFECTIVE INSTRUCTION?

We have been considering the kinds of learning experiences useful for attaining various types of objectives. These learning experiences have been considered in terms of their characteristics but not in terms of their organization. Since learning experiences must be put together to form some kind of coherent program, it is necessary for us now to consider the procedures for organizing learning experiences into units, courses, and programs.

What is Meant by "Organization"

Important changes in human behavior are not produced overnight. No single learning experience has a very profound influence upon the learner. Changes in ways of thinking, in fundamental habits, in major operating concepts, in attitudes, in abiding interests and the like, develop slowly. It is only after months and years that we are able to see major educational objectives taking marked concrete shape. In some respects educational experiences produce their effects in the way water dripping upon a stone wears it away. In a day or a week or a month there is no appreciable change in the stone, but over a period of years definite erosion is noted. Correspondingly, by the cumulation of educational experiences profound changes are brought about in the learner.

In order for educational experiences to produce a cumulative effect, they must be so organized as to reinforce each other. Organization is thus seen as an important problem in curriculum development because it greatly influences the efficiency of instruction and the degree to which major educational changes are brought about in the learners.

In considering the organization of learning experiences we may examine their relationship over time and also from one area to another. These two kinds of relationships are referred to as the vertical and the horizontal relations. When we examine the relationship between the experiences provided in fifth-grade geography and in sixth-grade geography we are considering the vertical organization, whereas when we consider the relationship between the experiences in fifth-grade geography and in fifth-grade history, we are considering the horizontal organization of learning experiences. Both of these aspects of relationships are important in determining the cumulative effect of educational experiences. If the experiences provided in the sixth grade in geography properly build upon the experiences provided in the fifth grade, there will be greater depth and breadth in the development of geographic concepts, skills, and the like. If the experiences in fifth-grade geography are appropriately related to the experiences in the fifth-grade history they may reinforce each other, provide for larger significance and greater unity of view, and thus be a more effective educational program; whereas, if the experiences are in conflict they may nullify each other, or if they have no appreciable connection, the student develops compartmentalized learnings which are not related to each other in any effective way when dealing with his own everyday life.

Criteria for Effective Organization

There are three major criteria to be met in building an effectively organized group of learning experiences. These are: continuity, sequence, and integration. Continuity refers to the vertical reiteration of major curriculum elements. For example, if in the social studies the development of skills in reading social studies material is an important objective, it is necessary to see that there is recurring and continuing opportunity for these skills to be practiced and developed. This means that over time the same kinds of skills will be brought into continuing operation. In similar fashion, if an objective in science is to develop a meaningful concept of energy, it is important that this concept be dealt with again and again in various parts of the science course. Continuity is thus seen to be a major factor in effective vertical organization.

Sequence is related to continuity but goes beyond it. It is possible for a major curriculum element to recur again and again but merely at the same level so that there is no progressive development of understanding or skill or attitude or some other factor. Sequence as a criterion emphasizes the importance of having each successive experience build upon the preceding one but to go more broadly and deeply into the matters involved. For example, sequence in the development of reading skills in social studies would involve the provision for increasingly more complex social studies material, increasing breadth in the operation of the skills involved in reading these materials, and increasing depth of analysis so that the sixth-grade social studies program would not simply reiterate the reading skills involved in the fifth grade but would go into them more broadly and deeply. Correspondingly, sequential development of a concept of energy in the natural sciences would require that each successive treatment of energy would help the student to understand with greater breadth and depth the meaning of the term "energy" in its broader and deeper connotations. Sequence emphasizes not duplication, but rather higher levels of treatment with each successive learning experience.

Integration refers to the horizontal relationship of curriculum experiences. The organization of these experiences should be such that they help the student increasingly to get a unified view and to unify his behavior in relation to the elements dealt with. For example, in developing skill in handling quantitative problems in arithmetic, it is also important to consider the ways in which these skills can be effectively utilized in social studies, in science, in shop and other fields so that they are not developed simply as isolated behaviors to be used in a single course but are increasingly part of the total capacities of the student to use in the varied situations of his daily life. Correspondingly, in developing concepts in the social studies it is important to see how these ideas can be related to work going on in other subject fields so that increasingly there is unity in the student's outlooks, skills, attitudes and the like.

These three criteria, continuity, sequence, and integration, are the basic guiding criteria in the building of an effective scheme of organization of learning experiences. To achieve them involves several problems which will be considered further.

Elements to Be Organized

In working out a plan of organization for a curriculum, it is necessary to identify the elements of that curriculum which serve as the organizing threads. For example, in the field of mathematics the organizing elements have frequently been concepts and skills. That is to say, mathematics teachers have identified certain basic concepts in mathematics of such major importance that they have become elements to be developed beginning in the early years of the mathematics program and extending through to the later years of the curriculum. For example, the concept of "place values" in a number system represents a very basic idea in understanding our methods of addition, subtraction, multiplication, and division. This concept is understood at a relatively low level by the fourth-grade child but can be developed into a much broader and deeper concept by the end of the ninth or tenth grade. This would be one element that could serve as an organizing element in achieving continuity and sequence. This element might also be a useful element in developing integration since the concept of the place value of a number system might be carried over to appropriate applications in shop, in social studies, in science and in other fields. Correspondingly, a skill in mathematics may be the ability to solve problems involving common fractions. This skill may be developed at a relatively low level in the seventh grade and may become increasingly deeper and broader in its implications and operations through the high school or college. Hence, this element too may serve as a thread in the organization of learning experiences.

In planning the curriculum for any school or any field, it is necessary to decide on the types of elements which most effectively serve as threads to use in the organization. The following is a good example of the work of a curriculum committee in identifying major types of elements that serve as the organizing elements for the curriculum in the social studies. This is a recent report of the Social Studies Curriculum Committee of the Dalton Schools in New York City.

"The Committee on the Social Studies has developed a list of common elements of the social studies curriculum that can serve as the threads running from the nursery-primary through the middle school and the high school to provide the basis for continuity, for sequence, and for integration in the curriculum. The Committee identified three kinds of common elements: concepts, values, and skills. To illustrate, the widely-used concept of interdependence of peoples is a concept which runs throughout the social studies curriculum. In the nursery-primary, the child begins to recognize his dependence upon other children in setting the table for lunch and their dependence upon him. He also recognizes interdependence with the milkman or the grocer. This concept grows more broadly and deeply until in the high school something of the interdependence of peoples of all nations in economic, social, political, intellectual, and aesthetic spheres is comprehended.

"To illustrate an element classified under values, consider

'respect for the dignity and worth of every human being regardless of race, nationality, occupation, income, or class.' This is a value that the Committee believes children should come to cherish, a value that they begin to experience in the primary grades where consideration for other children looms large and which is experienced at broader and deeper levels year after year in the school.

"As an illustration of a skill, the ability to make reasonable interpretations of social data could be cited. Simple social data are encountered by children in the primary grades and they learn to avoid bias and wishful thinking in their interpretations. As children move through the school, the data may become more complex but so do the procedures for careful interpretation. Hence, this is also an element that helps to give continuity and sequence to the social studies curriculum.

"Such elements also serve as threads that weave a more integrated curriculum. The concept of interdependence, for example, has implications in other fields as well as social studies—in art, in science, in English, in physical education, and so on. The value of 'the dignity and worth of every human being' is a value to be given consideration in the other subjects. Skill in interpreting social data may also be used or related to somewhat similar skills in science, in mathematics, in literature. Hence, these elements can be considered by teachers in other fields as possible threads for weaving a more closely integrated, total school experience as well as serving to give continuity and sequence year after year to the student's experience in the social studies.

"The Committee therefore urges each member of the faculty to examine this list of elements and to see how they are now or could be brought into his own teaching. Emphasis upon such common elements can improve the educational effectiveness of the Dalton Schools by increasing the degree of integration.

Tentative List of Common Elements in the
Social Studies Curriculum

A. *Concepts*
  1. Regarding individual 'human nature.'
    1.1 There are basic human needs which individuals seek to satisfy. All human beings have certain common needs but there is variety in their manifestation and attainment.
    1.2 The underlying motivation of a person has strong effects both on him and on others. Among the motives that have had great social consequence are:
      1.21 Struggle for survival.
      1.22 Desire to get ahead, to excel others.
      1.23 Quest for security.
      1.24 Struggle for freedom.
      1.25 Desire to attain one's ideals and aspirations for a better life.
    1.3 Much of our talk and action arises from unconscious motivation.
    1.4 Frustrations in human life have serious consequences. Fears, compensations, defences, inadequacies, compulsive behavior, and prejudices limit individual and social effectiveness.
    1.5 Although some individual characteristics are largely the result of inborn factors, many of the most important traits are acquired, much of the 'self' and individual personality are formed by experience and training.
    1.6 Human beings are almost infinitely teachable. In a sense 'human nature' is being changed every day.
    1.7 Ideals can be dynamic in human progress, especially when they are continuously clarified,

       reinterpreted and reapplied in changing stituations.

2. Regarding man and his physical environment.

    2.1 Space is an important dimension in human affairs, for location affects resources, ease of transportation and communication, and many physcial conditions of living.

    2.2 Time is an important dimension in human affairs, for events have roots and consequences and developments (changes) which require time.

    2.3 Climate, land features and natural resources have profound effects on man. Development, use and conservation of resources strongly influence his life and future.

    2.4 Man can influence his physical environment.

3. Regarding man and his social environment.

    3.1 Man forms social institutions and organizations to satisfy his needs.

    3.2 People are interdependent.

        3.21 The distribution of world resources makes for interdependence.

        3.22 Specialization and division of labor make for interdependence.

        3.23 The limitations of individual effort make for interdependence.

        3.24 Such universal human needs as affection, need to belong to a social group, need for respect from others make for interdependence.

    3.3 Social groups develop patterns for group living, thus producing customs, cultures, civilization, and society.

    3.4 Increasing knowledge and invention produce ideas and technology that disrupt some previous social arrangements. There is social lag in making adjustments to these disrupting forces. Hence:

3.41 Society involves both change and continuity. Both are inevitable, normal and serve useful social ends.

3.42 The idea of progress is not a continuous straight-line development. There are some regressions and cessations of advance.

3.43 Some far-reaching and rapid disruptions lead to revolution rather than evolution.

    3.431 Intellectual revolutions

    3.432 Political revolutions

    3.433 Economic revolutions

        (The Industrial Revolution)

3.5 An effective social group must provide both for individual needs to be satisfied and for integrated productive group activity. Hence, group organization involves problems of:

3.51 Achieving a balance of freedom and control.

3.52 The place and limits of compromise in dealing with conflicts of personal and social values.

3.53 Ethical and moral standards for the individual and the group.

3.54 The place of religions in individual and group life.

3.55 The place of the arts.

3.56 Democratic social groups in contrast to autocratic, aristocratic, or fascistic ones.

3.6 The organization of social groups for the production and distribution of goods and services has taken several forms and involves serious problems.

3.61 Nomadic life.

  3.62 Agriculture and family manufactures.

  3.63 Manorial systems.

  3.64 Mercantilism.

  3.65 Capitalism.

  3.66 Socialism.

  3.67 Monopoly and oligopoly.

 3.7 The organization of political units affects and is affected by economic organization. It has taken several forms and involves serious problems.

  3.71 Patriarchal clan or tribe.

  3.72 City-state.

  3.73 Feudalism.

  3.74 Ecclesiastical state.

  3.75 Nationalism and Imperialism.

  3.76 Democracy.

  3.77 Communism.

  3.78 Fascism.

 3.8 Social groups can be reshaped to fulfill their functions more adequately.

B. *Values*

 1. Attitudes toward self.

  1.1 Growing from self-love to self-respect; acceptance of self, realization of one's own worth.

  1.2 Integrity, honesty and frankness with self; objectively critical of self.

  1.3 Hopefulness for the future.

  1.4 Willingness for adventure; sense of mission, of reformation, of great crusade.

  1.5 Desire to make a productive contribution, not to be a parasite.

 2. Attitudes towards others.

  2.1 Respect for the dignity and worth of every human being, regardless of his racial, national, economic or social status.

    2.2 Cherishing variety in people, opinions, acts.

    2.3 Equality of opportunity for all.

    2.4 Tolerance, goodwill, kindliness.

    2.5 Desire for justice for all.

3. Attitudes toward social groups to which he belongs.

    3.1 Loyality to world society and world order.

    3.2 Acceptance of social responsibility.

    3.3 Willingness to submit one's problems to group study and group judgment.

    3.4 Balance of integrity of individual and group participation.

    3.5 Loyalty to social purposes of the group rather than undiscriminating loyalty to whatever the group does.

    3.6 Willingness to work for an abundance of the good things of life for all peoples in the world.

4. Intellectual and aesthetic values.

    4.1 Love of truth, however disconcerting it may be.

    4.2 Respect for work well done, worth of socially directed effort as well as achievement.

    4.3 Freedom of thought, expression and worship.

    4.4 Love of beauty in art, in surroundings, in the lives of people.

    4.5 Respect for reasonable procedures rather than force as the only proper and workable way of getting along together.

C. *Skill, Abilities and Habits*

1. In analyzing problems.

2. In collecting facts and other data.

    2.1 Skill in selecting dependable sources of data.

    2.2 Ability to observe carefully and listen attentively.

    2.3 Ability to read critically.

    2.4 Ability to discriminate important from unimportant facts.

2.5 Ability to take notes.

2.6 Ability to read charts, graphs, tables, and maps.

3. In organizing and interpreting data.

   3.1 Skill in outlining.

   3.2 Skill in summarizing.

   3.3 Ability to make reasonable interpretations.

4. In presenting the results of study.

   4.1 Skill in writing a clear, well-organized and interesting paper.

   4.2 Skill in presenting an oral report.

   4.3 Ability to prepare a bibliography.

   4.4 Ability to prepare charts, graphs, tables, and maps.

   4.5 Ability to write a critical book review.

5. Ability to do independent thinking.

6. Ability to analyze argument and propaganda.

7. Ability to participate effectively in group work.

8. Good work habits—planning of time, efficient use of time.

9. Ability to interpret a social situation, to recognize motives and needs of others.

10. Ability to foresee consequences of proposed actions.

"The foregoing elements have been stated frequently in technical terms and at the level represented by their mature development. Obviously, the intial introduction of the concept, value or skill with young children will be with those rudiments of the element that are appropriate for relative immaturity. Ultimately, it will be useful to prepare a statement regarding the aspects of these elements that can appropriately be introduced at each maturity level.

"It should also be clear that these elements are not to be viewed as single things, each to be a separate goal of instruction. Good teaching always involves a synthesis of several elements. The same learning experience can contribute to several of these elements at the same time—the child may in this learning experience deepen several concepts, gain a greater concern for certain social values, and acquire increased skill in study. The foregoing elements are suggested threads for the weaving; but the teaching will involve the closely woven fabric. The report will have been of value if it helps to weave a better integrated cloth."

The preceding report illustrates the work of a committee in identifying elements that are to serve as the organizing threads on which to build the curriculum or part of the curriculum. The illustration suggests too that these elements are major long-range items and not specific facts or specific habits or highly particularized matters which would not permit of development over the years and would not provide opportunity for extensive relationships to various other fields in the school curriculum. In working on the curriculum in any field, it will be necessary to identify elements that are relevant to and significant matters for that field as well as for the total curriculum. Then, of course, when the organizing elements have been selected they are to be used so as to provide for continuity, sequence and integration. That is, these elements should be planned to appear throughout the length and breadth of the instructional program.

Organizing Principles

It is not only necessary to recognize that learning experiences need to be organized to achieve continuity, sequence, and integration, and that major elements must be identified to serve as organizing threads for these learning experiences, it is also essential to identify the organizing principles by which these threads shall be woven together. For example, the concept of the interdependence of all peoples may begin in the primary grades with a recognition on the part of the learner that he is dependent upon his parents, upon

the milkman, and upon others, and they in turn are dependent upon him in certain limited respects. How shall this
concept then be broadened and deepened to provide for
greater sequence and integration over the years? One organizing principle might be to extend the concept by increasing the range of persons which the student recognizes
as being interdependent with him. For example, he may
extend his concept of interdependence to include people in
other cities, in other states, and in other nations. Another
organizing principle might be the extension of this concept
so as to broaden the range of respects in which people are
interdependent. That is, to recognize interdependence in
economic matters, interdependence in social matters, interdependence in aesthetic matters and the like. No doubt
both of these organizing principles as well as others may
be required to provide an adequate basis for developing this
important concept over the years, but these two principles
illustrate the problem involved. Organizing principles are
needed that can serve as a basis for planning the respects in
which the broadening and the deepening of major curriculum elements in the program will take place.

In identifying important organizing principles, it is necessary to note that the criteria, continuity, sequence, and
integration apply to the experiences of the learner and not
to the way in which these matters may be viewed by some-
one already in command of the elements to be learned.
Thus, continuity involves the recurring emphasis in the
learner's experience upon these particular elements; sequence refers to the increasing breadth and depth of the
learner's development; and integration refers to the
learner's increased unity of behavior in relating to the elements involved. This means that the organizing principles
need to be considered in terms of their psychological significance to the learner.

Over the years there has been a general recognition of the

distinction between logical and psychological organization. When such a distinction is made, it is an effort to point out the difference between the relationship of curriculum elements as viewed by an expert in the field and the relationship as it may appear to the learner. No doubt there are many cases in which a logical organization, that is, a relationship which has meaning and significance to an expert in the field, is also an appropriate psychological organization, that is, it can be a scheme of development in relations meaningful to the learner himself. On the other hand, there are times when sharp differentiation can be made between the connections seen by the expert in the field and the developments which are meaningful to the learner himself.

One of the most common principles of organization used in school curricula is the chronological. On this basis, for example, history courses are commonly organized so that the student sees the development of events over time. Although this is an easy scheme of organization for other fields, like literature, art, social studies, it needs to be examined pretty carefully to see whether it really provides the psychological organization which broadens and deepens the learner's command of the elements involved in this organization. Quite frequently a chronological organization is not satisfactory from this point of view.

Other organizing principles commonly used include: increasing breadth of application, increasing range of activities included, the use of description followed by analysis, the development of specific illustrations followed by broader and broader principles to explain these illustrations, and the attempt to build an increasingly unified world picture from specific parts which are first built into larger and larger wholes. Since there are so many possible organizing principles, it is important that in working upon any particular curriculum possible principles of organization are examined and decisions made tentatively to be checked by actual tryout of the material to see how far these principles prove satisfactory in developing continuity, sequence and integration.

The Organizing Structure

Thus far we have been considering the ways of putting experiences together so as to provide for effective organization. It is also necessary to consider the main structural elements in which the learning experiences are to be organized. Structural elements exist at several levels. At the largest level of the structural elements may be made up of (a) specific subjects, like geography, arithmetic, history, handwriting, spelling, and the like, or (b) broad fields, like social studies, the language arts, mathematics, the natural sciences, and the like, or (c) a core curriculum for general education combined with broad fields or with specific subjects or (d) a completely undifferentiated structure in which the total program is treated as a unit, as is found, for example, in some of the curricula of the less formal educational institutions, like the Boy Scouts or recreation groups.

At the intermediate level, the possible structures are (a) courses organized as sequences, such as social science I, social science II, social science III, when these three courses are definitely planned as a unifying sequence, or (b) courses that are single semester or year units without being planned or considered as part of a longer time sequence. In the latter category would be ancient history in the tenth grade, modern European history in the eleventh grade, and American history in the twelfth grade, when each of these courses is treated as a discrete unit not having a part-whole relationship to the total history program. Correspondingly, typical ninth-grade algebra does not build upon eighth-grade arithmetic, nor does tenth-grade geometry build upon ninth-grade algebra so that we can think of these courses as discrete unit courses rather than viewing them as a sequential organization at the intermediate level.

At the lowest level of organization, we have structures of several possible sorts. (a) Historically, the most widely used structure at the lowest level was "the lesson" in which a single day was treated as a discrete unit and the lesson plans for that day were more or less separate from other lessons which were planned for other days. (b) A second common structure is "the topic" which may last for several days or several weeks. (c) Increasingly, a third type of structural organization is to be found at this lowest level, commonly called "the unit." The unit usually includes experiences covering several weeks and is organized around problems or major student purposes.

So far as the present evidence is concerned, it appears that each of these different organizing structures may have certain values under different conditions. However, it is possible to indicate some of the advantages and disadvantages of each of these organizing structures. From the standpoint of the achievement of continuity and sequence the discrete subjects, the discrete courses for each semester or year, and the discrete lessons all impose difficulties that make vertical organization less likely to occur. There are too many boundary lines from one structure to another to assure of easy transition. Vertical organization is facilitated when the courses are organized over a period of years in larger units and in a larger general framework.

Correspondingly, to achieve integration is difficult if the organizing structure is composed of many specific pieces, since the tendency is to arrange the elements of each piece into some more unified form, but to work out the relationship of each of the pieces to each other becomes more difficult as more pieces are involved. Thus, fifteen or sixteen specific subjects in the elementary school present more hazards in achieving integration than an organization which has four or five broad fields like the language arts, the social studies, health and physical education and the like. A core curriculum provides even less difficulty in achieving integration so far as the interposition of boundaries between subjects is concerned.

So far as promoting a relationship to life is concerned, the point is frequently made that the kinds of problems encountered in life and the kind of life-like situations in which students might be expected to apply what they have learned in school tend to cut across narrow subject lines, which again argues for the use of broader groupings, like broad fields or core programs, rather than very narrow units, like many specific courses and subjects.

From the standpoint of achieving desirable organization, any structural arrangement that provides for larger blocks of time under which planning may go on has an advantage over a structural organization which cuts up the total time into many specific units, each of which has to be planned with some kind of transition and consideration of the work of other units.

At the other extreme, an undifferentiated organization of the school day imposes certain difficulties. The fact that various types of competence are desired in the school faculty and the fact that children need to shift from one activity to another before they become fatigued make it necessary to divide the school day into periods of varied activity and providing contact with more than one adult. This variety is likely to be more difficult in a structure that involves a completely undifferentiated organization.

The Process of Planning a Unit of Organization

The previous sections indicate the kind of problems faced in developing an effective organization of learning experiences and they suggest principles useful in attacking these problems successfully. Let us also note the methods of planning that are increasingly in use in the development of organized curriculum programs.

Although a great many ways of attacking the development of organization are now in use, in general, they involve the following steps: (1) Agreeing upon the general scheme of organization; that is, whether specific subjects, broad fields, or core programs are to be used. (2) Agreeing upon the general organizing principles to be followed within each of the fields decided on. This may mean, for example, that in mathematics the general scheme adopted involves an increasing abstraction of algebraic, arithmetic, and geometric elements which are treated together year after year in place of the principle of treating arithmetic elements first, then algebraic, and finally geometric. Or, it may mean an agreement in the social studies on the development of problems beginning with the community and moving out into the wider world rather than the decision on the use of organizing principles based upon purely chronological considerations. (3) Agreeing upon the kind of low level unit to be used, whether it shall be by daily lessons or by sequential topics or by teaching units. (4) Developing flexible plans or so-called "source units" which will be in the hands of each teacher as he works with a particular group. (5) Using pupil-teacher planning for the particular activities carried on by a particular class. This general operational procedure is increasingly used by various curriculum groups.

The development of preliminary flexible plans or so-called "source units" has as its purpose the provision of a great deal of possible material from which the teacher can select that to be used with any particular group. These plans are flexible enough so that they permit modification in the light of the needs, interests, and abilities of any group; and they are inclusive enough to cover a wide range of

possible experiences from which those that are most appropriate for a given group may be selected. A typical source
unit includes a statement of major objectives expected to
be obtained from the kinds of learning experiences outlined, a description of a variety of experiences that can be
used in attaining these objectives, an outline in some detail
of the culminating experiences that can be used to help
the student at the end to integrate and organize what he
has got from the unit, a list of source materials that will
help in the development of the unit, including books and
other references, slides, radio programs, pictures, record-
ings, and the like, and an indication of the expected level
of development of the major elements that operate as the
organizing elements in this particular curriculum. This
is necessary to prevent duplication on the one hand, and to
avoid undue omissions or big jumps in student development on the other hand, which are too great for the student
to attain.

In outlining the suggested learning experiences it is very
necessary not only to consider experiences that are inher-
ently related to the organizing principle of the unit but
also to care for the varying needs and interests of the individuals likely to be in this grade and also to provide for
each individual learner variety enough to stimulate continuing interest and attention and to prevent boredom. In listing source materials it is essential to recognize the varied
kinds of materials that can be used, not only the verbal but
the non-verbal ones, not only those that can be used within
the school but those that can be used at home, on field trips,
in community activities and the like. It is also important
to recognize the significance of culminating experiences
which help to tie together the varied experiences provided
throughout the unit. This facilitates integration and aids
the student in organizing his own understanding, attitude,
and behavior generally.

It is difficult to suggest the possible schemes that may serve to organize source units. Some source units are organized around big ideas, but in the main, the more successful ones have been organized around problems, particularly in the sciences and the social studies. In the aesthetics field, teaching units have often been organized around something to be done, or in some cases, a series of appreciation experiences which are neither problems nor big ideas There is still opportunity for a great deal of creative work in developing highly effective schemes for constructing source units in the various fields of the school curriculum.

As the source unit represents the preplanning that has gone on, so a great deal of planning must also be carried on while the units are actually being used. Each group of children may represent differences in background, in particular interests, in needs, that will involve considerable variation from one group to another. The value of having pupils participate with teachers in planning the more particular things to be done by that class is largely in giving the student greater understanding and meaning to his learning experiences as well as increasing the likelihood of his being well motivated. During such pupil-teacher planning, selections of activities will be made from among the many suggestions appearing in the source unit and there may also be additions made where children see possibilities in the unit which were not foreseen by those who planned the original source unit. As a result, the particular plan followed by each group will represent some variation from the original source unit and will never include all the possible materials suggested in the source unit itself .

It can be seen that planning the organization of curriculum experiences involves both a great deal of preplanning and also planning as the work goes on, but it is only in this way that it is possible to get the greatest cumulative effect from the various learning experiences used.

HOW CAN THE EFFECTIVENESS OF LEARNING EXPERIENCES BE EVALUATED?

4

Since we have considered the operations involved in choosing and formulating educational objectives and in selecting and organizing learning experiences, it may appear that we have completed our analysis of curriculum development. Although the steps previously discussed provide the plans for the day by day work of the school, they do not complete the planning cycle. Evaluation is also an important operation in curriculum development.

The Need for Evaluation

The steps thus far outlined have provided us with learning experiences that have been checked against various criteria derived from educational psychology and from practical experience. We also have utilized criteria regarding the organization of these learning experiences. In a sense, then, certain preliminary evaluations have already been made of the learning experiences. We may refer to these as intermediate or preliminary stages of evaluation. The learning experiences have been checked to see that they are related to the objectives set up and to see that they provide for other important psychological principles, so far as these principles are known. However, this is not an adequate appraisal of the learning experiences planned for curriculum and instruction. The generalizations used as criteria against which to check the learning experiences are general principles applying to generalized characteristics of the learning experiences and they are not highly precise statements of the exact conditions to be met in providing for the learnings desired. Furthermore, any set of learning experiences involves a number of criteria each of which can only be approximated so that we can only predict in general or with a certain degree of accuracy the likelihood that these experiences will actually produce the effects desired. Finally, the actual teaching procedures involve a considerable number of variables including variations in individual students, the environmental conditions in which the learning goes on, the skill of the teacher in setting the conditions as they are planned, the personality characteristics of the teacher and the like. These many variables make it impossible to guarantee that the actual learning experiences provided are precisely those that are outlined in the learning units. Hence, it is important to make a more inclusive check as to whether these plans for learning experiences actually function to guide the teacher in producing the sort of outcomes desired. This is the purpose for evaluation and the reason why a process of evaluation is necessary after the plans themselves are developed.

It should be clear that evaluation then becomes a process for finding out how far the learning experiences as developed and organized are actually producing the desired results and the process of evaluation will involve identifying the strengths and weaknesses of the plans. This helps to check the validity of the basic hypotheses upon which the instructional program has been organized and developed, and it also checks the effectiveness of the particular instruments, that is, the teachers and other conditions that are being used to carry forward the instructional program. As a result of evaluation it is possible to note in what respects the curriculum is effective and in what respects it needs improvement.

Basic Notions Regarding Evaluation

The process of evaluation is essentially the process of determining to what extent the educational objectives are actually being realized by the program of curriculum and instruction. However, since educational objectives are essentially changes in human beings, that is, the objectives aimed at are to produce certain desirable changes in the behavior patterns of the student, then evaluation is the process for determining the degree to which these changes in behavior are actually taking place.

This conception of evaluation has two important aspects. In the first place, it implies that evaluation must appraise the behavior of students since it is change in these behaviors which is sought in education. In the second place, it implies that evaluation must involve more than a single appraisal at any one time since to see whether change has taken place, it is necessary to make an appraisal at an early point and other appraisals at later points to identify changes that may be occurring. On this basis, one is not able to evaluate an instructional program by testing students only at the end of the program. Without knowing where the students were a the beginning, it is not possible to tell how far changes have taken place. In some cases, it is possible that the students had made a good deal of progress on the objectives before they began the instructional program. In other cases it may very well be that the students have very little achievement before they begin instruction, and almost all of that noted at the end took place during the time the instruction went on. Hence, it is clear that an educational evaluation involves at least two appraisals—one taking place in the early part of the educational program and the other at some later point so that the change may be measured.

However, it is not enough to have only two appraisals in making an educational evaluation because some of the objectives aimed at may be acquired during an educational program and then be rapidly dissipated or forgotten. In order to have some estimate of the permanence of the learning, it is necessary to have still another point of evaluation which is made sometime after the instruction has been completed. Hence, schools and colleges are making follow-up studies of their graduates in order to get further evidence as to the permanence or impermanence of the learnings which may have been acquired during the time these young people were in school. This is a desirable part of the evaluation program. In fact, so far as frequency of evaluation is concerned, much can be said for at least an annual appraisal carried on year after year as the children move through the school so that a continuing record of progress can be obtained and evidence accumulated to indicate whether desirable objectives are being realized and to indicate places where these changes are not actually taking place.

Since evaluation involves getting evidence about behavior changes in the students, any valid evidence about behaviors that are desired as educational objectives provides an appropriate method of evaluation. This is important to recognize because many people think of evaluation as synonomous with the giving of paper and pencil tests. It is true that paper and pencil tests provide a practicable procedure for getting evidences about several kinds of student behavior. For example, if one wishes to find out what knowledge students have, it may be easily gotten from paper and pencil tests if the students are able to express their ideas in writing, or can read and check off various items in a multiple response test or other similar tests. As another illustration, paper and pencil tests are useful devices to get at the ability of students to analyze and deal effectively with various types of verbal problems, with vocabulary, with reading, and a number of other types of skills and abilities easily expressed in verbal form. However, there are a great many other kinds of desired behaviors which represent educational objectives that are not easily appraised by paper and pencil devices. For example, such an objective as personal-social adjustment is more easily and validly appraised through observations of children under conditions in which social relations are involved. Observations are also useful devices to get at habits and certain kinds of operational skills. Another method which is useful in evaluation is the interview which may throw light upon changes taking place in attitudes, in interests, in appreciations, and the like. Questionnaires sometimes serve to give evidence about interests, about attitudes, and about other types of behavior. The collection of actual products made by students is sometimes a useful way of getting evidence of behavior. For example, the collection of themes students have written may serve to give some evidence of the writing ability of students, or the paintings students have made in an art class may serve to give evidence of skill and possibly interests in this area. Objects made in the shop or in the clothing construction course are additional illustrations of the collection of samples of products as an evaluation device. Even records made for other purposes sometimes provide evidence of types of behavior or interest in terms of educational objectives. For example, books withdrawn from the library may provide some indication of reading interests. Menus checked in the cafeteria may provide some evidence of the eating habits of students. Health records may throw some light on health practices. These are all illustrations of the fact that there are many ways of getting evidence about behavior changes and that when we think of evaluation we are not talking about any single or even any two or three particular appraisal methods. Any way of getting valid evidence about the kinds of behavior represented by the educational objectives of the school or college is an appropriate evaluation procedure.

Sampling is another basic notion of evaluation. Sampling is involved in many points. For example, evaluation assumes that it is possible to estimate the typical reactions

of students by getting evidence about a sample of his reactions. We do not collect all the written work the students
have ever prepared in order to get some estimate of their
writing ability. We recognize it is possible to judge the
writing commonly to be expected from this student by
examining a proper sample of his writing. Correspondingly, with reference to a student's knowledge, we do not
ask him all the questions about all the facts, principles,
concepts and the like that may be involved in his education,
but rather we choose a sample of these things to question
him about and we infer from his reaction to this sample
how he might react to the total set of items that might be
involved in his knowledge. This holds for all types of
human behavior, attitudes, interests, intellectual skills,
appreciations, and the like. We assume that it is possible to
infer the person's characteristic performance by appraising
his reaction in a sample of situations where this reaction is
involved.

Sampling is not only involved in appraising the individual's behavior, but it may also be involved in appraising
the effectiveness of curriculum experiences in use with a
group of students. It is not always necessary to find out the
reaction of every individual in order to see the effect that
the curriculum is producing. It is possible to take a sample
of students, and if this sample is properly chosen the results
with this sample of students may within small limits of
error properly represent the kind of results which would
have been obtained had all the students been involved in
the appraisal. Thus, it is possible for an appraisal to be so
designed that not too many students need to be interviewed
or probed with time-consuming means in order to get some
indication of what is happening to the students in terms of
the behavior appraised by these means. Correspondingly,
when follow-up studies are made to determine the per-
manency of the learning, it is possible to select a sample of

graduates that will be properly representative of the total group and to concentrate at fairly intensive study of the behavior of the sample of graduates in order to draw some conclusions about the permanence of learning which is probably characteristic of the average graduate of the program.

These are some of the basic notions regarding evaluation which guide in the development of an evaluation program. There are other notions involved in evaluation but these are among the most important ones. Their implications will be considered further as we examine the procedures for making an educational evaluation.

Evaluation Procedures

The process of evaluation begins with the objectives of the educational program. Since the purpose is to see how far these objectives are actually being realized, it is necessary to have evaluation procedures that will give evidence about each of the kinds of behavior implied by each of the major educational objectives. If, for example, one of the objectives is to acquire important knowledge about contemporary social problems, then it is necessary that the evaluation give some evidence of the knowledge students are acquiring. If another is to develop methods of analyzing social problems and appraising proposed solutions of them, then it is necessary that the evaluation procedures give us some evidence as to the skill of the student in analyzing social problems and appraising suggested solutions to them. This means that the two-dimensional analysis which served as a basis for planning the learning experiences also serves as the basis for planning the evalution procedures. The two-dimensional analysis of objectives thus serves as a set of specifications for evaluation. Each of the behavioral headings in the analysis indicates the kind of behavior which should be appraised to see how far that kind of behavior is developing; and each of the content headings of the analysis indicates the content to be sampled in connection with the behavior appraisal. Thus, in the case of the objectives regarding knowledge about social problems, the two-dimensional analysis indicates that evaluation of knowledge must be made for the behavior, and the content headings indicate what areas of knowledge should be sampled in order to have a satisfactory appraisal of the knowledge being acquired by the students in this field. Correspondingly, an objective, "Developing Interests in Literature," would require an appraisal of developing interests in students for the behavior aspect, and the content headings would indicate the areas in which interests might be expected to be developed and which should be sampled in order to see whether such interests are actually being developed. In this way a two-dimensional analysis of objectives becomes a guide to the evaluation of the curriculum.

It is, of course, assumed that these "behavioral objectives" have been clearly defined by the curriculum worker. They should have been defined clearly so as to provide a concrete guide in the selection and planning of learning experiences. If they have not yet been clearly defined, it is absolutely essential that they be defined in order to make an evaluation since unless there is some clear conception of the sort of behavior implied by the objectives, one has no way of telling what kind of behavior to look for in the students in order to see to what degree these objectives are being realized. This means that the process of evaluation may force persons who have not previously clarified their objectives to a further process of clarification. Definition of objectives, then, is an important step in evaluation.

The next step in evaluation procedure is to identify the situations which will give the student the chance to express the behavior that is implied by the educational objectives. The only way that we can tell whether students have ac-

quired given types of behavior is to give them an opportunity to show this behavior. This means that we must find
situations which not only permit the expression of the
behavior but actually encourage or evoke this behavior.
We are then in a position to observe the degree to which
the objectives are actually being realized. In some cases, it is
easy to see the kinds of situations that give students the
chance to express desired types of behavior. We are ac-
customed to stimulating students to express ideas through
questions and it is therefore possible in the question situation to evoke reactions of the students that involve knowledge and ability to deal with verbal materials. When we
consider the whole range of desired objectives, we can see
that the situations are not all of this type. If we are going
to see how children are developing personal-social adjustment, we must use those situations which give children a
chance to react to other children. This may mean looking
for evidence about personal-social adjustment in the nursery school during those periods when children are playing
and working together. It may mean that we shall look for
evidences of interests in those situations where there is
opportunity for free choice of activity. Students may, therefore, freely express their interests. If we want evidence of
the student's ability to express himself orally, we must look
in those situations which evoke oral expression. The principle is simple enough that any evaluation situation is the
kind of situation that gives an opportunity for the sudents
to express the type of behavior we are trying to appraise.
Although the principle is simple, there are still many
problems involved in finding situations that are sufficiently
under control and permit the teacher or other evaluator to
have access to them in order to see the types of behaviors the
students are developing. In case some situations are difficult
to handle, then one of the tasks of the specialist in evaluation is to try to find other simpler situations that will have

a high correlation with the result obtained when the situation is used which directly evokes the kind of behavior to be appraised.

It is only after the objectives have been identified, clearly defined, and situations listed which give opportunity for the expression of the behavior desired that it is possible to examine available evaluation instruments to see how far they may serve the evaluation purposes desired. It is not really possible to look at a particular test and to decide whether it would do for appraising a certain educational program until the objectives of the program have been identified and defined and until the kinds of situations that would give an opportunity for this behavior to be expressed have also been identified. After these steps have been taken, one can then examine particular tests and see how far they sample the types of objectives that are to be appraised and how far the tests either use situations which directly evoke the kind of behavior to be appraised or else use situations which have been correlated with the situations that directly evoke the type of behavior. It has too commonly been true that persons have gone to test catalogues or have looked at sample tests and selected them without having these previous steps in mind to serve as the basis for making a wise selection. Just because Test A is the most widely used test in physics or Test B is commonly recommended for art or Test C has been prepared by some widely known specialist in mathematics, these are not indications that these tests may be appropriate ways of getting evidence about the particular objectives that are aimed at in a given educational program. It is very necessary to check each proposed evaluation device against the objectives that are being aimed at and to see whether it uses situations likely to evoke the sort of behavior which is desired as educational objectives.

When available evaluation instruments are checked in

this way, it is quite probable that the curriculum constructor will find that there are available instruments that will be quite satisfactory for certain of the educational objectives, that there are other available instruments which can be modified somewhat and made appropriate for certain other educational objectives, and finally, that there are some educational objectives for which no available evaluation instruments can properly be used. For these last, it may be necessary to construct or devise methods for getting evidence about the student's attainment of these objectives. The construction of evaluation instruments can be a very difficult task if the purpose is to get a highly refined instrument, but a great deal can be done of a less refined sort by collecting evidence in rather simple ways relating to these various educational objectives. We shall discuss illustrations of these a little later.

If it is necessary to construct an evaluation instrument for a particular objective, the next step is actually to try out some of the situations suggested as situations that give the student a chance to express the behavior desired. This try-out provides an opportunity to see whether these situations will serve as convenient ways of getting evidence. Thus, it may appear that the type of situation likely to give students a chance to show their ability to analyze problems is a situation in which a number of problems are presented in written form and the students are asked to analyze them. Situations of this sort can actually be tried out with students to see how far the responses obtained provide an adequate basis for checking the student's ability to analyze problems. Or, a situation that is likely to give students a chance to indicate their interests is to present a questionnaire in which a variety of activities are listed and the students are asked to check those in which they are interested and also to mark those in which they have no interest. If this appears to be a situation likely to give students an opportunity to show interests, then it should be used in trial form to see how satisfactorily it works. This step is a useful step in developing possible evaluation devices into forms where they can be satisfactorily used.

After deciding on certain situations used to get evidence about the behavior of students, it is then necessary to devise a means of getting a record of the student's behavior in this test situation. In the case of a written examination the student makes his own record in his writing. Hence, the problem of getting a record of his behavior is not a serious one. On the other hand, a situation that gives nursery school children a chance to play and work together may be a good situation to provide evidence of personal-social adjustment but it is necessary to get some record of the children's reaction in this situation if there is to be opportunity to appraise this reaction after it has been made. This may involve making a detailed description of reaction by an observer, it may suggest the use of a motion picture or sound recording, it may suggest the use of an observer's check list by which he checks off particular types of behavior that commonly appear or it may involve some other means of getting a satisfactory record of the children's reaction. This is a step that must be considered in connection with each test situation to be sure that the situation not only evokes the desired behavior but that a record can be obtained which can be appraised later.

The next step in developing an evaluation instrument is to decide upon the terms or units that will be used to summarize or to appraise the record of behavior obtained. This method of appraising the behavior should, of course, parallel the implications of the objective itself. For example, if reading interests as an educational objective are to be defined as the development of increasingly broad and mature interests, it then becomes necessary to decide upon units by which a record of children's reading can be summarized to indicate breadth and to indicate maturity. Breadth may be indicated by a number which measures the different categories of reading material included in the youngster's reading for the year. Thus, a child who reads only Wild West stories and detective stories would have his reading list classified under two categories only and the figure 2 would represent a measure of breadth. This would be in contrast to a boy whose reading record could be classified under four categories such as adventure, romance, psychological, sociological. The fact that the second boy read materials classified under a wider number of categories would be represented by the number 4 in contrast to the number 2. Correspondingly, if different reading levels can be classified under different levels of maturity, it becomes possible to summarize a reading record in terms of its average level of maturity and thus to provide a measure of that aspect of reading interest. This illustration has been chosen because it is very different from the problem as it is usually viewed by the person who reads and scores the test; and, yet, essentially all evaluation involves this problem, that is, the decision upon the characteristics that are to be appraised in the behavior and the unit to be used in the measurement or summarization of these characteristics. In the case of reading interests, the characteristics used were range and maturity so that the methods of summarization provided a rating for range and maturity.

The problem is a similar one in summarizing a typical objective type test. Suppose it is a measure of knowledge. The question then to be faced is: Will knowledge be summarized in terms of the number of different items in the sample which the student was able to remember properly, or is it better indicated by some classification of the items so as to indicate which topics he remembers best and which less well, or is there some other way by which the objective of knowledge can be most satisfactorily summarized or appraised in order to serve the purpose of evaluation? Every kind of human behavior which is appraised for its part as an educational objective must be summarized or measured in some terms and the decision about these terms is an important problem in the development and use of evaluation instruments.

It should be clear that for most purposes the appraisal of human behavior should be an analytic one rather than a single score summary. Simply to know that John Smith made a score of 97 and Mary Jones made a score of 64 on some evaluation instrument used is not an adequate kind of summary likely to be most helpful for improving the curriculum. It is much more useful to have summaries which indicate the kinds of strengths and weaknesses, summaries at least in terms of each objective; and in many cases it may be desirable to have several scores or summaries for each objective so as to describe more adequately the achievement of this particular sort of objective. Thus, it is useful to know whether the students are making progress in developing a range of reading interests even though they may be making less progress in developing maturity of reading interests. It is helpful to know that students are making progress in their skill of interpretation in reading although their reading interests may not be as satisfactory as hoped. This kind of analytic summary which indicates particular strengths and weaknesses is, of course, invaluable in using the results to improve the curriculum. It means that the plan for appraisal must be developed before scoring and rating is actually made. Decisions about these points are necessary decisions in developing an evaluation program.

The next step in the construction of an evaluation instrument is to determine how far these rating or summarizing methods are objective, that is, to what degree two different persons, presumably competent, would be able to reach similar scores or summaries when they had an opportunity to score or summarize the same records of behavior. If the scores or summaries vary markedly, depending upon who does the scoring or summarizing, it is clearly a subjective kind of appraisal and requires improvement in its objectivity in order to be a more satisfactory means of appraising a human behavior. Sometimes improvement can be made through clarifying the specifications for scoring, sometimes through getting a more refined record of behavior itself. It is beyond the scope of the present discussion to outline the various techniques for refining and improving the objectivity of the instruments. It is necessary, however, to recognize this problem and to attempt to get a more objective procedure when necessary. When these possible evaluation instruments have been tried out, one cannot only check on the objectivity of the scoring or summary but also check upon the adequacy of the sample of behavior included in the instrument. In general, the size of the sample of behavior to be obtained depends upon how variable that behavior is. If one wishes to get evidence about the social attitudes of students and these attitudes are highly consistent in each individual, it takes only a few samples to get a rather dependable indication of the attitude of each student. On the other hand, if there is wide variability in each student's attitudes, for example, if he is highly selfish at some points and highly social at others, it takes a much larger sample of his behavior in order to infer reliably about the degree of his social or selfish attitudes. Hence, it is not possible to be sure in advance how large a sample of behavior must be collected regarding a given objective in order to have a dependable sample from which to draw conclusions about the individual's status. It is possible after trying out an instrument to find out what the variation among the items in the instrument is and thus to estimate how reliable the sample is and whether a larger or smaller sample would do satisfactorily. This is the problem of reliability of a test or other evaluation device; and, although it is beyond the scope of this discussion to describe methods of estimating reliability, it is important to recognize what reliability means and to realize that if a given test is too short to provide an adequate sample or if a given set of observations does not cover a large enough span of time to get an adequate sample of the student's behavior, it will be necessary to extend the sample before dependable conclusions can be drawn.

Since we have used the two terms for two of the important criteria for an evaluation instrument, namely, objectivity and reliability, it is necessary to emphasize the third and most important criteria of an evaluation instrument, namely, validity. Validity applies to the method and indicates the degree to which an evaluation device actually provides evidence of the behavior desired. Validity can be assured in one of two ways. One way is by getting directly a sample of the kind of behavior to be measured, as when one observes directly the food children are selecting as the basis for inferring food habits, or one obtains an actual record of reading done as an indication of reading habits, or one presents problems for children to analyze to get evidence of their ability to analyze problems. This is known as "face validity"—the evaluation instrument is valid on the face of it because it directly samples the kind of behavior which it is desired to appraise. The other way of assuring validity is through correlating a particular evaluation device with the result obtained by a directly valid measure. If it can be shown that the results of a certain reading questionnaire correlate very highly with the results obtained from an actual record of reading, then the reading questionnaire might be used as a valid indication of what children read. It would be valid because the results are shown by experimental methods to correlate highly with the direct evidence. In some cases, persons developing tests find that it is expensive or difficult or otherwise impracticable to get evidence by the direct method and they try out various possible ways for getting evidence which are simpler and easier to handle. None of these should be used, however, as a valid instrument until it has been shown to correlate highly with the evidence obtained directly, that is, from an instrument which has face validity.

These steps indicate the procedures followed in making an evaluation and in developing an instrument for an evaluation. In case the instrument is found to have too little objectivity or reliability, it is necessary to improve it. It is also necessary to make any other revisions indicated by the preliminary tryout, such as eliminating ambiguities in directions, dropping out parts of the instrument which got no significant reactions from students. In general, then, the result is a continually improved instrument for getting evidence about the degree to which students are attaining given educational objectives.

These instruments are used in order to obtain summarized or appraised results. These results may be in the form of scores, or descriptions, or both, depending upon the form which can be most satisfactorily used to summarize the behavior in terms that are appropriate for the objectives desired.

Using the Results of Evaluation

Since every educational program involves several objectives and since for almost every objective there will be several scores or descriptive terms used to summarize the behavior of students in relation to this objective, it follows that the results obtained from evaluation instruments will not be a single score or a single descriptive term but an analyzed profile or a comprehensive set of descriptive terms indicating the present student achievement. These scores or descriptive terms should, of course, be comparable to those used at a preceding date so that it is possible to indicate change taking place and one can then see whether or not educational progress is actually happening. If it is found, for example, that the range of students' interests in reading is no greater at the end of the tenth grade than it was at the end of the ninth grade, it is clear that no appreciable change is taking place in reading interest. Correspondingly, if it is shown that the ability to interpret reading passages critically is no higher at the end of the tenth grade than at the end of the ninth grade, again, no educational change is taking place. It is, therefore, essential to compare the results obtained from the several evaluation instruments before and after given periods in order to estimate the amount of change taking place. The fact that these are complex comparisons, that they involve a number of points and not a single score, may complicate the process, but it is necessary for the kind of identification of strengths and weaknesses that will help to indicate where the curriculum may need improvement. For example, in connection with one curriculum program which involved the development of a core focused upon contemporary social problems, it was found that at the end of the first year, the students had acquired a great deal more information about these contemporary problems, that they had shifted their social attitudes slightly in the direction of greater social and less selfish attitudes, but that their attitudes were much more confused and inconsistent than before, that they had not gained any skill in analyzing social problems, and that their ability to interpret social data was worse because the students were drawing more unwarranted conclusions than before. Putting all of these things together gave the teachers the chance to see the kinds of strengths, which were largely covering more material and more ideas, and the kinds of weaknesses, which had to do with their greater inconsistencies, less ability to analyze critically and the like. This is more helpful in getting at the seat of the difficulty in this particular core curriculum than if there had been a single score which indicated a small amount of improvement but did not analyze this improvement into a number of different categories.

It is not only desirable to analyze the results of an evaluation to indicate the various strengths and weaknesses, but it is also necessary to examine these data to suggest possible explanations or hypotheses about the reason for this particular pattern of strengths and weaknesses. In the case just cited, after examining all the data available, it is suggested that this implied that a great deal more ground was covered and that not enough time was being spent in careful critical analysis. This was checked against the actual amount of reading provided which turned out to be more than 6,000 pages and the number of social problems dealt with, which turned out to be twenty-one, both of which in the light of these data seemed to be excessive and suggested that a possible explanation for these weaknesses was that too much material was being covered and not enough time devoted to critical analysis, interpretation, and application.

When hypotheses have been suggested that might possibly explain the evaluation data, the next step is to check those hypotheses against the present available data, that is, against additional data that may be available, and to see whether the hypotheses are consistent with all the data then available. If they appear to be consistent with the available data, the next step is to modify the curriculum in the direction implied by the hypotheses and then to teach the material to see whether there is any actual improvement in student achievement when these modifications are made. If there is, then it would suggest that the hypotheses are likely explanations and the basis for improving the curriculum has been identified. In the case just cited it was possible to reorganize the course for the coming year and to reduce the number of major problems from twenty-one to seven and to reduce the quantity of reading material by more than half so as to utilize more time in interpreting, applying, analyzing, and otherwise treating the material dealt with. At the end of the second year, it was found that, although the students had not gained quite so much in the range of information acquired, they had gained greater consistency in social attitudes, had gained greater skill in analyzing social problems, and had become able to draw better generalizations from the data presented to them. This would indicate that the hypothesis that what was wrong with the course was that it covered too much ground seemed to be a sound one. This is a typical procedure that can be followed in using evaluation results so as to modify and improve the curriculum and instructional program.

What is implied in all of this is that curriculum planning is a continuous process and that as materials and procedures are developed, they are tried out, their results appraised, their inadequacies identified, suggested improvements indicated; there is replanning, redevelopment and then reappraisal; and in this kind of continuing cycle, it is possible for the curriculum and instructional program to be continuously improved over the years. In this way we may hope to have an increasingly more effective educational program rather than depending so much upon hit and miss judgment as a basis for curriculum development.

Other Values and Uses of Evaluation Procedures

In the foregoing discussion of evaluation, we have concentrated primarily upon the use of evaluation procedures in identifying the strengths and weaknesses of the curriculum program. This is its main function in curriculum work. It also serves other purposes. The very fact that it is not possible to make an evaluation until objectives are clearly enough defined so that one can recognize the behavior to be sought means that evaluation is a powerful device for clarifying educational objectives if they have not already been clarified in the curriculum planning process.

Evaluation also has a powerful influence upon learning. It has been shown in the New York Regents' Inquiry that the Regents' examinations which are the evaluation instruments of the state have more effect upon what is taught in New York State than course of study outlines as such. Students are influenced in their study by the kind of evaluation to be made and even teachers are influenced in their emphasis by the sort of evaluation which they expect to be made. This means that unless the evaluation procedure closely parallels the educational objectives of the curriculum the evaluation procedure may become the focus of the students' attention and even of the teachers' attention rather than the curriculum objectives set up. Hence, evaluation and curriculum must be closely integrated so that the effect will not be for the curriculum planning to be ignored in order for diverse objectives appraised by evaluation to be given major attention.

Evaluation procedures also have great importance in the individual guidance of pupils. It is not only valuable to know about students' background but also to know about their achievement of various kinds of objectives in order to have a better notion of both their needs and their capabilities. Any comprehensive evaluation program provides information about individual students that can be of great value.

Evaluation can also be used continuously during the year as a basis for identifying particular points needing further attention with particular groups of students and as a basis for giving individual help or planning individual programs for students in the light of their particular progress in the educational program.

Finally, evaluation becomes one of the important ways of providing information about the success of the school to the school's clientele. Ultimately, schools need to be appraised in terms of their effectiveness in attaining important objectives. This means that ultimately evaluation results need to be translated in terms that will be understandable to parents and the public generally. Only as we can describe more accurately the results we are attaining from the curriculum are we in a position to get the most intelligent support for the educational program of the school. Neither parents nor the public can be satisfied long with reports about the number of children enrolled and the number of new buildings built and things of that sort. Eventually, parents have a right to know what kind of changes are being brought about in their children. Now, most of the reports of this sort that they get are from appraisals that are not fairly made. We hear about the number of persons rejected because of lack of reading ability or lack of physical health in connection with Selective Service, but we have no means of tracing those cases back to particular schools. Increasingly, we must expect to use evaluation procedures to determine what changes are actually taking place in students and where we are achieving our curriculum objectives and where we must make still further modifications in order to get an effective educational program.

HOW A SCHOOL OR
COLLEGE STAFF MAY WORK
ON CURRICULUM BUILDING

Thus far this syllabus has dealt with the problems of planning a program of instruction from the point of view of the students examining its purposes, functions and structure in order to get a rational picture of their interrelations. Specific attention has not been given to the way in which a particular school or college might apply this rationale in rebuilding its curriculum. In many cases the applications will be obvious, particularly when an entire school staff is agreed upon the need for constructing a new instructional program. On the other hand, there are many situations in which a total reconstruction of the curriculum is not contemplated and yet this rationale can be appropriately applied in a systematic attack on a part of the program.

If a school-wide program of curriculum reconstruction is undertaken, it is necessary that there be widespread faculty participation. The instructional program actually operates in terms of the learning experiences which the students have. Unless the objectives are clearly understood by each teacher, unless he is familiar with the kinds of learning experiences that can be used to attain these objectives, and unless he is able to guide the activities of students so that they will get these experiences, the educational program will not be an effective instrument for promoting the aims of the school. Hence, every teacher needs to participate in curriculum planning at least to the extent of gaining an adequate understanding of these ends and means.

In a small faculty, the staff may work as a committee of the whole in conducting studies of the learners, studies of life outside the school and in examining the reports of subject specialists. The entire staff, when small, may also operate as a committee of the whole to formulate its philosophy of education and to work out a statement of psychology of learning. Then the staff, as a whole, can use these results in selecting the objectives for the school. They can also conduct their deliberations in the group as a whole regarding the general organizing framework to be used. Finally, the planning of learning experiences for particular courses will normally be done by those who are to teach them, but even in this step, teachers of the same subject at other grade levels and teachers in related fields will be found helpful in planning. Furthermore, the staff as a whole, when small, may serve as a reviewing committee for these detailed plans. A similar procedure is applicable to the planning of the evaluation program.

Larger schools will find it necessary to operate as special committees, some making studies of the learner, others studying contemporary life, others examining reports of subject specialists. Drafting committees may be used to formulate initial drafts of philosophy and psychology, but these drafts will need to be studied, discussed and revised as a result of consideration by the entire staff. For such deliberations the staff will usually divide into groups small enough for active discussion. The selection of objectives and the deliberations regarding the general organizing framework to be used can also be done by one or more committees, then reviewed by the entire staff. As with smaller staffs, the planning of learning experiences for particular courses can be participated in by all those who are to teach them, and each planning group may also include teachers of the same subject at other grade levels, and teachers in related fields. However, special reviewing committees will need to be formed to review and coordinate the detailed instructional plans.

Although a school-wide attack is preferable in getting a

rational revision of the curriculum, improvements can be made if only a part of the instructional program can be dealt with. Thus, curriculum building can be undertaken for a single subject like mathematics, or a single grade, like the ninth, or even for the courses offered by an individual teacher. Within the limits in which the curriculum is to be rebuilt, the same general rationale can be used. However, a partial attack must be planned with relation to the other parts of the instructional program which are not to be modified.

Another question arising in the attempt at curriculum revision by a school or part of a school is whether the sequence of steps to be followed should be the same as the order of presentation in this syllabus. The answer is clearly "No." The concern of the staff, the problems already identified, the available data are all factors to consider in deciding on the initial point of attack. In one school, participation by the staff in a program of child study may provide an entering wedge in studying the learner, in another school the results of a follow-up of graduates may focus attention upon identifiable inadequacies in the present program which will lead easily to systematic study. In another situation, the deliberations over a school philosophy may provide an initial step to an improvement of objectives, and then to a study of the learning experiences. The purpose of the rationale is to give a view of the elements that are involved in a program of instruction and their necessary interrelations. The program may be improved by attacks beginning at any point, providing the resulting modifications are followed through the related elements until eventually all aspects of the curriculum have been studied and revised.